EGYPT

People

Gods

Pharaohs

Rose-Marie & Rainer Hagen

EGYPT

People

Gods

Pharaohs

TASCHEN

Page 2: Statue of Ramesses II, temple of Luxor
Page 6: Bangle of king Shoshonk I from Tanis (detail)
Pages 8/9: The Sphinx, Giza
Pages 10/11: Nile scenery
Pages 12/13: Riders in front of the Pyramids of Giza

© 1999 Benedikt Taschen Verlag GmbH
Hohenzollernring 53, 50672–Köln

Edited by Susanne Uppenbrock, Cologne
Design: Kühle und Mozer, Cologne
Cover design: Angelika Taschen, Cologne
English translation: Penelope Hesleden,
Beverley, UK and Ingrid Taylor, Munich

Printed in Italy
ISBN 3-8228-7058-7
GB

Contents

Foreword

People have always built pyramid-shaped structures, examples in our own time being a hotel in Las Vegas and the glass entrance to a museum in Paris. However, apart from this ingenious building form, many other things conceived and developed in the kingdom of the pharaohs are still up-to-date today – the new pyramids are merely the most visible.

Even now we still do not fully understand how these gigantic tombs commemorating the pharaohs were erected. What we do know, at least to a large extent, is how the people who built them lived, what pleased those early Egyptians, what excited them and what they believed about the world around them. Tomb pictures bring it all alive before our eyes, and accounts deciphered by Egyptologists of events such as the strike of the tombworkers tell us about everyday life, the administrative system and how disputes were settled.

Little changed in the course of the 3,000 years of Ancient Egyptian history, at least in comparison to the last 2,000 years of European history, and in particular the last 200 years. Pharaohs and gods came and went but the Egyptian vision of the underworld, their system of government and level of technology remained largely unchanged. And then there was always the major issue of food, which was completely dependent on the recurring floods of the Nile. On account of this remarkable stability we have decided not to write about Ancient Egypt in chronological order. Dates are mentioned, but only as background information. Anyone requiring an overview of the division into kingdoms and dynasties and the reigns of the most important kings will find it on pp. 232–235.

One of the Ancient Egyptians' most outstanding achievements was the development of a script and to give this a high profile we have scattered hieroglyphs throughout each chapter. It is also the theme of three chapters – in the chapter on scribes we look at the privileged position of those who could write, in the chapter on writing, we explain the Egyptian system of symbols, a much more complex system than our alphabet, and in the final chapter we tell the story of the hard work and sheer luck which led to the hitherto unknown symbols finally being deciphered.

Further reading is listed on page 237. This book aims to answer some basic questions about life in Ancient Egypt and whet your appetite to find out more. We could not have written it without the help and encouragement of the staff of the Egyptology department at the University of Hamburg and in particular Mrs Muriel Elsholz. We would like to express our warm thanks to them.

The Authors

The Nile, the fertile river banks, the desert – this is how we picture Egypt from Aswan in the south to Cairo in the north, where the Delta begins. But only four per cent of the entire country is inhabited and fertile – Egypt is a river oasis in a desert state.

A Gift of the Nile

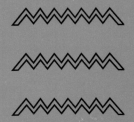

mu = water

Egypt owes its existence to a single river. "Egypt", wrote the Greek traveller Herodotus in about 450 B.C., "is a gift of the Nile". Without the Nile early advanced civilisation would not have developed, without the Nile we would not have our contemporary state.

On the other hand, however, the country as a whole is a desert state, with only around four per cent of its area cultivable and habitable. The habitable part – from Aswan to Cairo – is like an oversized river oasis, in some places scarcely a hundred metres wide, in others stretching for several kilometres into the arid region of the Sahara. North of Cairo the Delta begins; the river splits into several branches and the people no longer live on either side of the bank, but in between the waters. The region is fertile; twice as much is grown in the Delta as between Cairo and Aswan.

The Nile feeds the land and for thousands of years it even determined the rhythm of the year. At the time of the summer solstice a great inundation approached from the south, reaching the mouth a month later. For about three months it caused the Nile to overflow its banks, flooding the oasis and the Delta. Afterwards, in October and November, sowing and planting took place and from January to April the fruits and cereals ripened and were harvested.

In order to use the water as productively as possible, the Egyptians created an elaborate system of canals and terraced fields. Not only did the Nile bring vital moisture, it also washed the salt from the ground, rinsing the dirt away. It brought with it mud rich in minerals, which gave the land its colour and made it fertile. The black earth was called Kemet. The Egyptians also called their country, their state, Kemet.

Rainfall in the south is equally non-existent and very scarce in the Delta area; the harvest depended entirely on the height of the annual summer inundation. If it was favourable, Egypt produced an abundance of corn and could lay in stocks and export the rest. Too much or too little rain for several successive years led to catastrophic famine.

Not only did the Egyptians live on the Nile, they also lived with it. The summer inundation was by far the most important event as far their material existence was concerned. It was measured in at least 20 places; some of the Nilometers – a flight of steps with height markings – can still be seen today. The measurements served as forecasts of the size of the harvest and also, we presume, for calculating annual taxes.

The situation changed with the building of the Aswan dams – the first was opened in 1902, the last and highest in 1971. The mass of water could now be spread over the whole year, the cultivable areas extended and the number of harvests increased. Moreover, the hydroelectric power station in Aswan produces a quarter of Egypt's power requirements. However, in the dammed-up water reservoir, Lake Nasser,

Until 1902, when the first dam was built at Aswan, the Nile burst its banks annually from the south, inundating the river valley. This 19th century photo shows the Pyramids of Giza in the background.

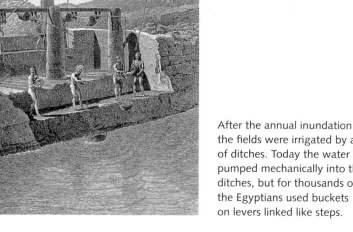

After the annual inundation the fields were irrigated by a system of ditches. Today the water is pumped mechanically into the ditches, but for thousands of years the Egyptians used buckets on levers linked like steps.

the mineral substances sink to the bottom and the natural fertilisers of the prolific country have had to be replaced by industrial products. In addition, water cleansed of mud flows faster, carrying away bank reinforcements, and the water table rises, threatening old buildings. In fact, it seems today as if this large-scale interference with nature has brought just as many disadvantages as advantages.

The Ancient Egyptians had discovered neither the sources of the Nile nor the causes of the inundation. Herodotus explains, "I have been unable to learn anything about the nature of the Nile either from the priests or anywhere else. I would have dearly liked to know the reasons for the flooding of the Nile [...] no Egyptian [...] could answer my question, why the reverse is true of the Nile than of any other river." By reverse, he meant that it floods in the middle of summer and not after the snow melts. It was not until the 19th century that explorers reached the headwaters and discovered that at over 6,700 kilometres, the Nile is the

In 1838 the French architect Hector Horeau published a depiction of the Nile in perspective showing some of the most important edifices. In the foreground is Pompey's pillar in Alexandria, above it the Pyramids of Giza and Saqqara, then among other buildings the Ramesseum. The temples of Karnak and Luxor can be seen on the opposite side of the Nile and at the top is the rock temple of Abu Simbel.

iteru = river

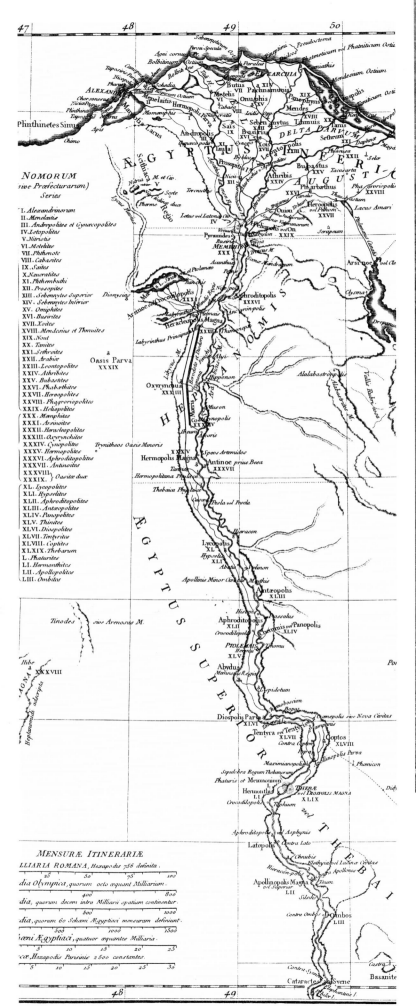

When the Nile, which rises in Nubia, reaches Egypt it has already flowed over 1,000 kilometres. The Egyptians did not know where the sources were; one lies in Ethiopia, another branch feeds from Lake Victoria, at equator level. Here is one of the river branches meandering through Uganda. The "Aegyptus Antiqua" map dates from 1765.

longest river in the world. It rises from the Blue Nile, which comes from the Ethiopian Highlands and from the White Nile, whose headwaters lie in southern Sudan and extend to Lake Victoria. They are fed by the regular tropical belt precipitation and the violent summer monsoon rains in Ethiopia.

The Great Highway

In Ancient Egypt, the Nile determined the rhythm of the year, food supplies and the mode of transportation. The river was the country's highway on which people travelled and goods were transported. When constructing large buildings such as the pyramids, the Egyptians first dug out an access canal as close as possible to the building site. From a traffic-engineering point of view they were a river society: the Egyptians developed many types of boats, mostly by lashing together papyrus plants, but they had no vehicles for transport on land. They did take over the light horse-drawn hunting chariots from the Hyksos, Asiatic interlopers who ruled the land between 1650 and 1550 B.C., but materials were still transported by donkey (and camels through the desert) or pulled on wooden sledges by oxen or people. Their disregard for the wheel as an aid to transport can be explained most easily by the fact that the river ruled the Egyptian way of thinking.

The Nile holds the country, over 1200 kilometres long, together, but it also divides it into two halves, east and west. For the Egyptians the two banks had a different significance: the sun rising in the east, made the eastern part the land of the living, while the west, where it sets, was the land of the dead. This division was not strictly adhered to, but is still very apparent in the former capital, Thebes (now Luxor). The quarters of the living lay on the east bank, while the graves of the kings, queens and high officials all lay on the west bank of the Nile; the ruling elite had their "houses" for life in the underworld built on the edge of the desert.

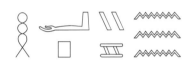

Hapi = God of the Nile, of the inundation

The blue Nile god Hapi is holding the central stem of a palm leaf in his hand. It is the character for "year" and symbolises the annual tidal wave, the height of which determined the harvest and thus the well-being of the population. On the right the fertility god is holding his hands over two expanses of water.
From the Book of the Dead of Any, 19th Dynasty, London, British Museum

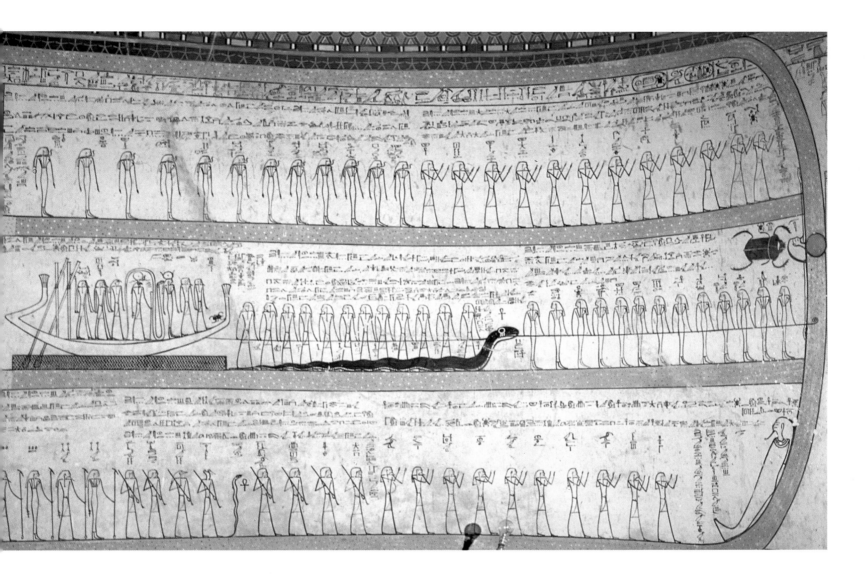

The River of the Gods

If Egypt was a gift of the Nile, then – for the Ancient Egyptians – the Nile was a gift of the gods. They gave or took away the water and one of the pharaoh's tasks was to speak respectfully to the Nile gods. At the same time, there was no exact delineation between river and god, as, for the Egyptians, the real world and the world of the gods were interwoven. The word Hapi makes this clear: it means the Nile, the flood water and at the same time God of the Nile. In Aswan they still knew of the pot-bellied river gods Krophi and Mophi, who sit under the rocks and make the water flow. It flows directly from the subterranean lakes of the Nun, the primeval waters from which the world came into being and on which the visible world is floating, so to speak. The Ancient Egyptians imagined that the Nile flowed back into its original waters and came out again in an eternal life cycle. "Hail, Nile, you who come out of the earth and return there, to give Egypt life [...]" says a hymn of worship. The river, which the Egyptians saw flowing by daily, not only determined their earthly life but also their whole imaginary world. The sun-god travelled across the heavens in a boat and at night came back to the east on the waters of the underworld. When the priests carried statues of gods in

Divine beings pull the barque of the sun god from west to east over the waters of the underworld at night. The sun is rejuvenated by the snake of the "life of the gods", rising anew in the sky in the morning. The symbol for the rejuvenated sun is the scarab. *Part of a wall-painting in the tomb of Tuthmosis III, Thebes, Valley of the Kings, New Kingdom, 18th Dynasty*

Under the rocks of the first cataract, the Nile god Hapi makes the waters flow out of his vessels. *Relief at the temple of Isis on the island of Philae, 2nd century A.D.*

processions, they sat in barques, as if they were moving on the river. Sandals and boats were put in the tomb with the dead for the dangerous journeys through the underworld. The sandals corresponded to the foot size of the deceased and there were small wooden or clay model ships, often manned by oarsmen, or sometimes full-size ships, as in the graves at the foot of the Cheops' Pyramid.

In 1954 the first of five ship-tombs was discovered near Cheops' Pyramid, containing a 43-metre-long rowing boat, capable of floating, broken down into its individual parts. Most of the wood was expensive Lebanese cedar, as the palms of the Nile valley were not suitable for boat building. The boards were held together by ropes, and rope and lengths of material for the cabin covers lay in the shaft. Today, this well-preserved boat, over 4000 years old, stands ready for use in its own museum directly above the place where it was found, a witness to the ship-building skills of the Ancient Egyptians and the influence of the Nile on how they imagined their underworld.

In the Egyptian's imagination the gods almost always moved on the water; in processions priests carried the divine statues in barques.
From the Book of the Dead of Chonsuju, New Kingdom, Vienna, Kunsthistorisches Museum

Catching fish with a trawl net between two papyrus boats. Behind them pleasure boats or boats for travelling in belonging to a prosperous man.
Wooden model from the tomb of Chancellor Meketra, 11th Dynasty, around 2000 B. C., Turin, Museo Egizio

depet = boat

This royal barque, capable of floating, is over 4,000 years old. It is 43 metres long and its 1,224 individual parts lay well-ordered and provided with building instructions in a tomb in front of the Cheops' Pyramid. The barque was discovered in 1954; today it stands in its own museum directly above the place where it was found.

In ancient times the famous
pyramids of Giza were counted
among the Seven Wonders of the
World. They were built between
2550 and 2490 B.C. as royal tombs,
the one in the foreground for
Mycerinus, the middle one for
Chephren and the one behind,
which is also the highest, for
Cheops. Pyramids offered
the embalmed bodies of the kings
protection from robbers and
made the ascent of their
souls to the stars easier.

The Pyramids –
Wonders of the World

mer = pyramid

In Egypt there were many stories about how the earth began.
According to one of them, before the beginning of time there
was neither earth nor sky, nor gods, but only water. In these
primeval waters mud gathered into a primeval mound and
on this hill life began.

The vision of land rising up out of water was a familiar one
to Egyptians, as they experienced it each year after the
inundation of the Nile. The pyramids symbolised for them
the very first rising up of the earth from its chaotic origins.
The pyramids were not only linked with the depths and
primeval waters, but also with the skies. Egyptians believed
their kings were gods or sons of gods and that after death
they rose up to the stars. The other gods "lift you up in their
arms", it says in a Pyramid text, "and you rise, oh King,
up to heaven and climb upwards as on a ladder". The pyramids were equivalent to ramps which helped the pharaohs in
their ascent. In more practical, earthly terms, the pyramids
also served as fortresses. They were intended to protect the
embalmed body of the king and the precious objects placed
in the tomb against robbers. According to Egyptian belief
the dead person lived on in the underworld and for this he
needed his earthly form: "Join your head to your bones and
join your bones to your head". He needs the body so that
the "soul" can unite with him, he needs the funerary objects
to feed him and enable him to live in fitting regal style.
Tombs were "houses for eternity". In order to protect the
deceased, the corridors within the pyramid were blocked by
heavy stones dropped into place and the entrances were
made undetectable from outside. Unlike other monumental
structures, pyramids had no visible entrance and as long as
the priests of the dead continued to carry out their duties
no-one dared to force their way in.

Djoser

King Djoser's tomb – a forerunner
of the classic pyramids – was built
around 2650 B. C. Djoser had united
Upper and Lower Egypt for the first
time, and perhaps due to his
outstanding importance the people
wanted to build him a monument
reaching up into the sky instead
of one of the low mastaba still
customary at that time. The base is
right-angled but not completely
square, as the later pyramids were.

From the Step Pyramid of Djoser onwards, the Egyptians felt their way by trial and error towards the classic pyramid shape. The Bent Pyramid of King Seneferu (built around 2570 B.C.) has a square outline, but the architect did not dare to persevere right to the top with the original angle of inclination. From halfway-up it was built at a lower angle.

The Step Pyramid of Djoser did not stand on its own, it was part of a tomb complex which was 544 metres long and 277 metres wide. It was surrounded by a high wall which has now been partly reconstructed.

Tombs of high officials and members of the royal family next to the Cheops' Pyramid. At the beginning of the Old Kingdom kings were also buried in or below low buildings such as these called "mastaba tombs".

Geometry and Architecture

Pyramids did not suddenly appear; their development stretches back a long way. At the beginning of the Old Kingdom, the kings were buried in square tomb constructions. These tombs contained a room for the coffin, chambers for supplies and hunting equipment, rooms in which the dead person could relax and also a space in which to place the sacrificial objects. The walls were made of brick made from dried Nile mud. From a distance these tombs resemble low benches, or in Arabic, mastabas, and so that was the name archaeologists gave to this style of tomb. The funerary complex of King Djoser, the founder of the Third Dynasty, was also planned as a mastaba, but it was the first to be built of stone and raised in a step-like structure. Its final height was 60 metres. The result was a stepped pyramid, on an almost square ground plan. The Step Pyramid was surrounded by various cult buildings and the complex as a whole was encompassed by a 10-metre-high wall. It was then the biggest funerary complex ever to have

been built. What was the reason for this? Under Djoser the empire had finally been united. He was the most powerful pharaoh Egypt had ever seen and his tomb was supposed to represent the earthly significance of the dead king. The man who was responsible for the step pyramid was Djoser's highest-ranking official, the vizier Imhotep. His name is closely linked to this new style and to a new dimension in royal tomb architecture. Imhotep was still revered right up to the New Kingdom, being regarded as the son of the god Ptah, the lord of all builders. The generations of architects following Imhotep filled out the steps of their kings' royal tombs to form smooth sloping surfaces and made the sides of the base all of equal length – thus producing the geometrical form of the pyramid. How steep such a form could be built was, however, not yet fully understood. The Bent Pyramid of King Seneferu makes this clear: at about 40 metres from the ground, the angle of inclination was changed and the pyramid completed at a shallower angle than originally intended. An earthquake is thought to have alarmed the builders and they feared the pyramid would collapse.

Forty Centuries in Stone

Seneferu's son was Cheops, who ruled from 2553 to 2530 B.C. For him the largest of all pyramids was erected, a structure 146 metres high. As a comparison, the Statue of Liberty in New York is 92 metres in height, the Taj Mahal in India 95 metres and St Peter's in Rome 129 metres. The Greeks counted Cheops' Pyramid among the Seven Wonders of the World and Napoleon, sitting watching his troops clamber up its sides, is said to have calculated that the stone used in the pyramid and the two neighbouring pyramids was enough to build a wall, three metres high and half-a-metre thick, around the whole of France. "Soldiers", he is said to have cried to his army, "Forty centuries are looking down on you!"

The upper ten metres of Cheops' Pyramid and the capstone are missing today. So, too, is the outer casing of light-coloured limestone, which is only preserved in one or two places. But the forces of nature are not what removed the tip and the cladding; that was done by later rulers and the people living nearby, in search of building materials. Caliph Abdullah el-Mamun, who ruled Egypt from 820 to 827, even wanted to tear the pyramid down completely to uncover the treasure still thought to be inside. He only abandoned this plan when calculations showed that the work would cost more than the sum total of taxes collected in Egypt! Instead he restricted himself to knocking through an entrance on the north side, the one used today. According to an Arab author writing several hundred years later, when the workers opened the pyramid they found a jar filled with 1000 gold coins. The caliph had "the sum calculated which had been spent on making the opening, and it showed that this was exactly equivalent to the amount of gold found. On hearing this he was amazed that they had known what he would spend [...]."

It was El-Mamun's workers who penetrated through into the burial chamber and who brought out the coffin. When it was opened, "one could see within it the corpse of a person dressed in golden armour studded with all kinds of jewels. On his breast lay the blade of a sword without a handle and next to his head a red hyacinth stone, the size of a hen's egg, which lit up like flames in a fire. El-Mamun took this stone for himself." Today the only movable object in Cheops' Pyramid is the heavy stone sarcophagus, which probably once contained the wooden coffin with the mummified remains of Cheops. The lid of the sarcophagus is missing and everything else has been removed from the pyramid, at least in the rooms so far accessible. These number three. A good thirty metres under the base of the pyramid is a chamber hewn out of the rock, but never fully completed and evidently never used. Perhaps there was too little oxygen in this space for the workers to breathe or lanterns to burn. A second, smaller chamber was also never finished, again for reasons unknown. A lack of oxygen cannot have been the problem, as this section lies above the level of the base.

The mighty Cheops' Pyramid rises above a rocky desert plateau. The sides measure 227.50 metres around the base, and it is 146.60 metres high. Today the top has gone and, except in a few places, the white Tura limestone is missing – those building in later times helped themselves to the valuable, ready-to-use materials.

Cheops was the architect of the highest pyramid. However, the only depiction of the king remaining is an ivory statue.
Cairo, Egyptian Museum

This chamber is called the Queen's Chamber, although there are no indications of a queen. Higher still is the King's Chamber with his sarcophagus: walls, ceilings and floor are made from blocks of pink granite, the walls are smoothly polished and the floor covers 60 square metres. Above the King's Chamber researchers have found five low roof chambers, each covered by mighty blocks of stone, which were probably integrated to divert the load from the pyramid above that point down past the chamber.

The most impressive part of the inside of the pyramid is the entrance to the King's Chamber called the Grand Gallery. This is a gently rising stepped hall, 27 metres long and as high as an average house, i.e. eight and a half metres. The walls are of polished sandstone and, from a height of two metres and above, the stones overlap, being placed ever closer together to create a kind of stepped roof. No drawing or photograph can give an accurate impression of this space. And it would be false to believe it had been built for public view – it was intended entirely for the king and for his eyes alone. It is a masterpiece of construction, within this already remarkable feat of architecture. After the burial of the king in the pyramid, giant blocks of granite were rolled down the ramp, thus closing them up for all time, as it was thought.

At the upper end of the Grand Gallery lies the burial chamber, which was robbed in the Middle Ages. Only a pink granite sarcophagus is left in which the wooden coffin of the embalmed king stands.

The cross-section through the Cheops' Pyramid shows three burial chambers, of which only the top one (3) was completed and put to use. Above it is a construction made of mighty blocks of stone (2), which were to divert the load that would otherwise weigh down on the chamber. Two shafts (1) lead from the burial chamber to the outside, providing an air supply and probably also easing the path of the king's soul to the stars. In front of the burial chamber is the Grand Gallery (4) with access to the "Queen's Chamber" (5). Underground lay what was presumably the oldest chamber (6).

iner = stone

The Grand Gallery conveys a quite extraordinary impression of space that cannot be captured by a camera. It is a stairwell, 47 metres long, whose ceiling is made up of several layers of overlapping stone blocks. In the "Description de l'Égypte" written by scientists on Napoleon's Egyptian expedition, it is depicted twice, once from above and once from the lower end.

Building Techniques – An Unsolved Mystery

There are no contemporary documents at all about how many people, what tools and what plans were used to build the pyramids. Perhaps they were destroyed over the centuries or maybe there never were any in the first place. Nor are there any written texts about the meaning and significance of the pyramids. Egyptologists have to draw their conclusions on the basis of the buildings themselves or from other contemporary texts.

It is easy to work out where the stones came from: pink granite came from Aswan, limestone (used for cladding the outside and sometimes the inside of pyramids) from Tura, infill material from the quarries of Giza on which Cheops' Pyramid stands. Aswan lies 800 kilometres upstream, Tura on the other bank of the Nile. Transport was by ship. Using canals and specially constructed landing stages, the freight was brought close to the building site. A ramp was then built of earth, brick and stone which led up from the landing stage a distance of 40 metres to the Giza plateau above. What is not known is how the Egyptians hoisted the building materials during actual construction work on the pyramids. They must have erected a second ramp which was gradually extended as the pyramid grew in size. There are two possibilities: either the ramp came from one side, or it wound around the four sides of the pyramid. Calculations show that if the side-ramp option had been used, by the time the pyramid was finished it would have contained more building material than was actually contained in the pyramid itself. The version winding around the pyramid uses less material, but covers up the part of the pyramid already completed, thus making it difficult to check edges and the angle of inclination. Which of these options the Egyptians actually used, or whether there was a third way, has not yet been established.

The stone blocks were probably transported on wooden sledges. Vehicles with wheels were unknown. Nor did they use horses to drag loads. Only oxen were used on the flat for pulling, but they can hardly have been suitable for work on the narrow ramps. Many of the blocks were over five tons in weight, and it would have taken around 50 workers to drag them upwards. Herodotus, the Greek historian who travelled to Egypt in around 450 B.C., wrote that the Egyptians had used lifting gear. But the information he received was already 2000 years old and recent research has shown no evidence for lifting appliances – only levers, rollers, crowbars and sleds. It is supposed that the stone blocks were roughly hewn into shape in the quarries and then given their final form when in place. The precision displayed in this work has given rise to much admiration. The English Egyptologist William Flinders Petrie compared them to the "accuracy of expert opticians". Up to this day the skills of these Ancient Egyptian stone masons remain unsurpassed.

Wheels were unknown in the Old and Middle Kingdoms, so heavy loads such as blocks of stone for constructing pyramids or sculpting monuments were pulled on sledges. Foremen beat time for the workers, while one of the workers moistened the guide way.
Reproduction of a wall-drawing, now destroyed, from the Middle Kingdom, published in 1824 in the book "Reise zur Oase des Jupiter Ammon" by the Prussian General Consul Baron Heinrich von Minutoli

How the pyramids were erected remains a mystery to this day. The Egyptians must have used ramps which grew with the building work and either came in from the sides or wound around the pyramids. There were no lifting appliances as we know them today. Oxen can hardly have been suitable for pulling on the ramps.

kat = construction

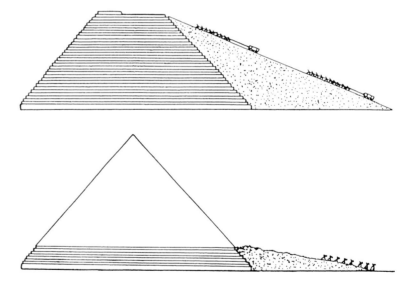

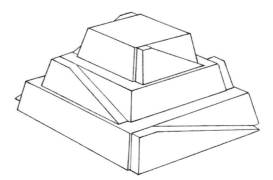

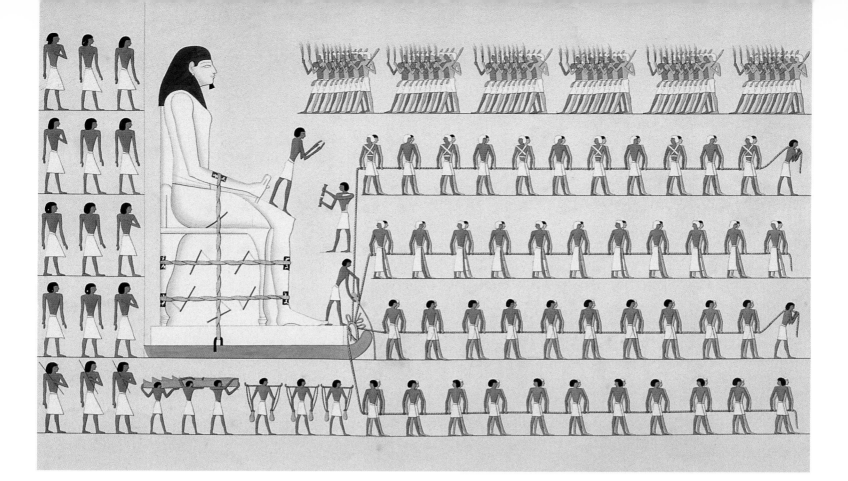

Their ability to turn geometric plans into reality was also highly developed. How else would they have succeeded in building such large constructions with exactly the same angle of inclination on all sides? Or building the pyramid form so perfectly that there was no "lean" to one side? One basic requirement (apart from protractors) was a level base. Spirit levels were unknown, but the principle was probably understood. A shallow trench was dug along the line of the four 230-metre-long sides of Cheops' Pyramid and corrected until the water in the trench was perfectly level. Contemporary documents about how work was organised on these sites are also lacking. The only figures we have date from Herodotus, 2000 years later: "100,000 people worked on them, and every three months these people were replaced", he wrote, and "recorded on the pyramid in Egyptian letters is the quantity of radishes, onions and garlic consumed by the workers. If I remember correctly, the sum named by the interpreter who told me what the inscriptions meant, was 1,600 talents of silver, […] construction work […] lasted twenty years." And ten years were needed for building the approach routes.

Today experts consider this to be a realistic estimate of how long Cheops' Pyramid would have taken to build. Yet it seems likely that the skilled stone masons would have worked throughout the year, not just for a part of it. And that the bulk of the labour force would probably not have been replaced every three months, but instead employed in full numbers for just three months of the year, during the inundation of the Nile, at a time when they were unable to work in the fields.

For Herodotus and the Egyptian priests from whom he obtained his information, building pyramids was forced labour and Cheops a tyrant who despised humanity. He is even said to have taken advantage of the charms of his own daughter: "Cheops was such a despicable person that when he was short of funds he took his own daughter to a house of ill-repute and ordered her to earn a certain amount of money there (how much the priests did not say). She managed to get the required amount of money together and decided that one day she, too, would have a monument made to herself. Each man who visited her was asked to bring her a stone to use in building the monument. These stones are said to have been built in the middle of the three pyramids which stand in front of the big pyramid […]."

As ridiculous as this anecdote may seem, it nevertheless attests to the bad reputation of King Cheops. Herodotus' informants evidently knew little of the glorious days of the Old Kingdom: Cheops was considered to be a god and Egypt and all its people his personal property. Whether on the fields, in the temple or in the palace they all worked for him, directly or indirectly, at all times. And when they helped construct a gigantic monument like a burial pyramid they were serving not only him but also themselves, for the pharaoh was the guarantor for the well-being of his people in the underworld.

The Sphinx – Guardian of the Pyramids

Construction work on a burial pyramid, or later a rock tomb, started immediately after a pharaoh was enthroned. The person responsible for the work was the highest-ranking official – Egyptologists called him a vizier, in line with Oriental custom. Cheops' vizier was Hemiunu, and in 1912, when his tomb was opened, one of the things found in it was a life-size statue of him, with the head missing. The shattered pieces of the head were found lying around on the floor – clearly tomb robbers had been at work smashing out the valuable metal or stones used for the eyes. Nevertheless Cheops' "governor of all royal building work" is still preserved as a life-size statue, albeit damaged, whereas the figure of Cheops himself is only known from a 5.5 cm high ivory statuette. This can be seen in the Egyptian Museum in Cairo.

Pyramids did not stand in isolation; they were part of a larger complex. The complex included the tombs of higher officials (like Hemiunu) and family members: Cheops' officials lay to the west of the pyramid in precisely aligned rows of mastaba tombs; his three wives each have a small pyramid on the east side. A temple, also part of the pyramid complex, was used for the daily cult of the dead, and the remains of its basalt floor are preserved on the east side of the pyramid. Leading down from the mortuary temple beside the pyramid to the valley temple was a covered walkway, which today lies beneath inhabited houses and is therefore out of reach to archaeologists for the time being. In the valley temple, sacrificial objects were placed for the deceased: fresh provisions for the long journey through the land of the dead, or for the priests who carried out the rituals of the cult and who watched over the tomb. The barques on which Cheops was to travel were stored in large shafts at the foot of the pyramid.

Next to the pyramid of Cheops stands that of his brother Chephren and of his son Mycerinus, both successors of Cheops. These pyramids are somewhat smaller but, together with Cheops' Pyramid and the mighty Sphinx of Chephren, they form one of the most famous architectural ensembles in the world. The Sphinx is 20 metres high and 73 metres long, hewn from a single block of stone: a lion's body with a pharaoh's head, recognisable as a pharaoh by the royal head-dress and the uraeus on its brow. The remains of the missing ceremonial beard can still be seen clearly. The Sphinx is visible for miles around in the desert sand – it was originally regarded as the protector of the pyramid complex, later revered as the embodiment of the sun god and later still feared by the Arabs as the "Father of Horror". However, the Sphinx was not always easy to see. Several times over the past millennia sand has practically buried the giant sculpture, leaving only the head sticking out. And at least twice during the time of the pharaohs it was dug out on divine instruction. The gods delivered their instructions through princes, who were assured of pharaoh status if they uncovered the Sphinx. An inscription on a stele between its paws tells what happened to Tuthmosis IV – he lay down to sleep in the shade of its stone head and heard "how the majesty of this wonderful god spoke with its own mouth, like a father speaks to a son […]."

There were advantages in the Sphinx's repeatedly being buried in sand, for it meant that the Arabs and the Mamelukes could only damage the head (the beard and nose are missing) and not the body. Rising ground water and air pollution are the factors causing damage today, through erosion, which is far more serious than the occasional misuse of the statue for target practice. With large chunks already broken away on the left front paw, on the shoulder and on the tail, this regal figure is turning into a long-term patient. Hollow sections inside the statue have been detected but are as yet still uninvestigated.

The clear signs of decay do not, however, detract from its charm and its continuing power to fire the imagination. The Sphinx is the model for many cult and legendary creatures. The Egyptians themselves later combined the lion's body with animal heads and the Greeks turned the male sphinx into a female form with wings which set riddles for travellers and ate the ones who could not solve them. A watchful guardian was thus turned into a highwayman, a patron into a demon. The Sphinx became a figure of the Romantic Age, and also of modern-day comic strips and horror films.

The Sphinx and Cheops' Pyramid have one thing in common – over the millennia they have awakened curiosity and a desire to explore the past, and they have fired the imagination, particularly of believers in esoteric lore. The latter dispute the theories of archaeologists, saying that the Great Gallery was a kind of planetarium, and that the basic dimensions of Cheops' Pyramid can be used to calculate the circumference of the Earth. They say, too, that the builders of Cheops' Pyramid had set out to construct a "monumental text book" of the entire knowledge of their time. And they say that the Sphinx was in no way a monument of the Old Kingdom, but originated in the days long before the Flood.

The Sphinx lies stern and unapproachable. 73 metres long and 20 metres high, it is made up of a lion's body and a pharaoh's head, a mythical creature that has preoccupied and unsettled man since ancient times in many manifestations. The uraeus on its brow and the ceremonial beard are missing and of the pharaoh's signs of office only the royal head-dress remains.

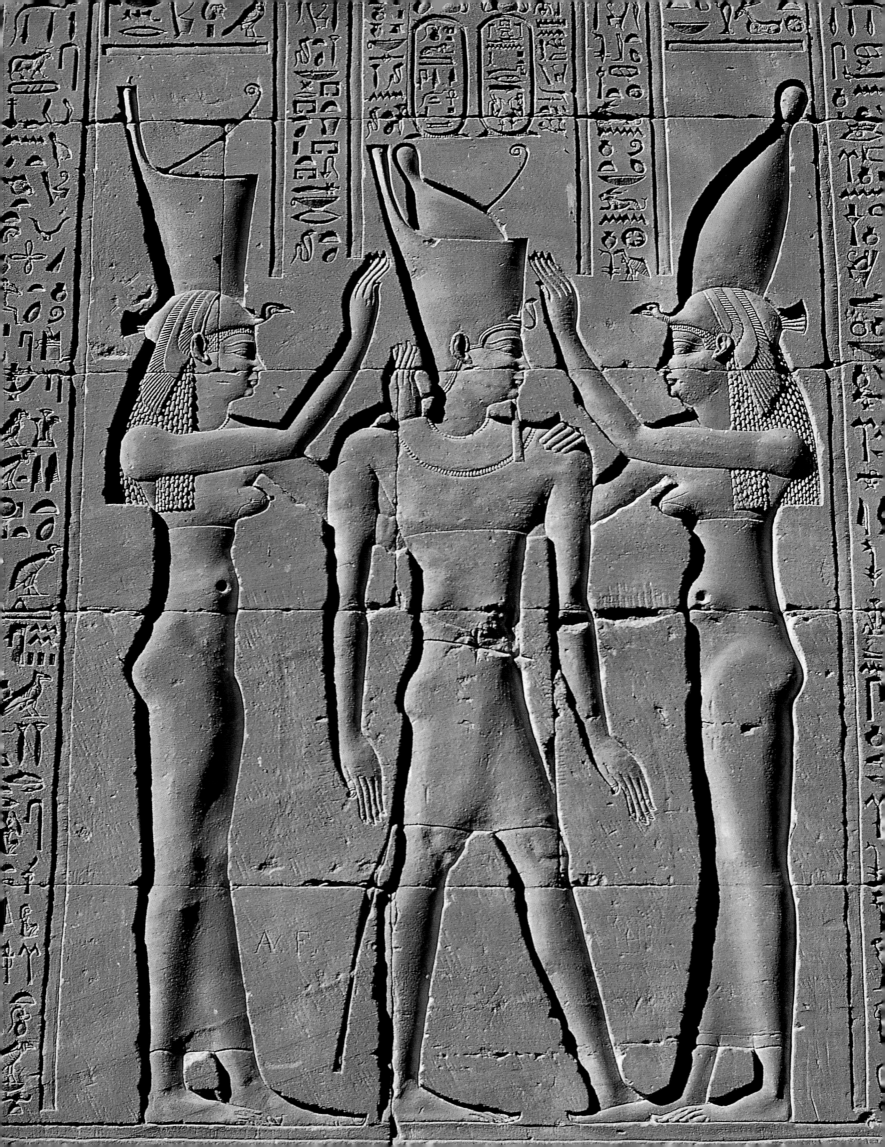

The goddess on the left is wearing
the crown of Lower Egypt, the one
on the right that of Upper Egypt.
They are crowning the pharaoh,
who unites the two crowns –
because the king must hold the two
halves of the country together,
preventing disputes and chaos.
*Relief from the Temple of Edfu,
181–145 B. C.*

The Pharaoh
Unites the Land

anch, udja, seneb
= may he live long, and remain hale
and hearty (this request always
accompanied pharaoh's names)

With raised club, the pharaoh is threatening his enemies, holding them captive by the hair and pushing them into the dust. This depiction of the king as victor can be found as a stone-carved relief a hundred times, in royal residences as well as at the borders and even as far as Nubia. The picture of the victorious pharaoh is not portraying an event, but a task – the pharaoh must protect Egypt. It is among the great achievements of Ancient Egyptian culture that it developed pictorial formulae for all the important tasks of rulers. The Egyptians could see on the temple walls what a pharaoh was and what he had to do. The very first task he had to carry out was to unite the two parts of the country. During the civil wars in the so-called Intermediate Periods (between the Old and the Middle, and the Middle and the New Kingdoms) this was no mythical task, but a real one – the Egyptians felt themselves to be threatened by chaos and it was up to the pharaoh to save them. The process was depicted by the uniting of Upper and Lower Egypt, represented by two plants, the papyrus and lotus, bundled together, or by two gods, mutually blessing the pharaoh. We can see how important the idea of unification was by the pharaoh's title; he was always and explicitly called "King of Upper and Lower Egypt".

Besides unification and defence, one of the most important tasks was maintaining internal order. Justice, truth and harmony were personified in the goddess Maat. She wears an upright feather on her head, and is occasionally represented by this feather alone. The pharaoh, bringing a small Maat to the gods on the palm of his hand, is showing that he is not misusing his power and that he is searching for the truth in cases of dispute among his subjects. "Treat Maat well while you are on earth," one king advises his son, "comfort those who weep, do not distress widows, do not drive anyone away from the property of his father, and do not undermine the position of any official. Be on your guard against unjust punishment and do not kill, for that cannot be beneficial to you." Professing Maat meant restricting the all-powerful king and she also obliged him to seek consensus with his subjects. Officials praise a pharaoh, saying "You make the laws for all eternity," and prudently add, "to the satisfaction of the people." Like many peoples, the Egyptians have traced the origin of their rulers back to divine forefathers, and at the beginning of the Old Kingdom the Egyptian kings were even regarded as gods. However, this halo slipped and from the 4th Dynasty the kings were regarded only as sons of the gods. The national god Amun, so it was said, always fathered the future king with the reigning pharaoh's wife by assuming the form of the pharaoh. As he was of a divine nature, he was also the highest priest in the land and responsible for contact with the gods.

The unity of Upper and Lower Egypt was not only symbolised by the double crown, but also by the binding together of the lotus and papyrus, the heraldic plants of the two parts of the country.
Relief at the base of the Colossi of Memnon, Thebes, 18th Dynasty

neb-taui = Lord of both countries

The particular sign of the goddess Maat is the ostrich feather on her head. Maat embodies order, justice and truth, and every pharaoh is beholden to her. Here, with her wings outstretched, she is protecting Queen Nefertari, wife of Ramesses II.
Wall-painting from the tomb of Nefertari, Valley of the Queens, New Kingdom, 19th Dynasty

One of the most important tasks of a pharaoh was defending the country. The Egyptians had never seen horses and chariots until they were occupied by the Hyksos at the end of the Middle Kingdom.
Stele, 18th Dynasty, Cairo, Egyptian Museum

away. The temple scribes liked to leave out weak or unworthy pharaohs, those unloved by the gods, so these did not pass into the Egyptian royal ideology.

The fact that the succession did not always take place according to the rules can only be determined indirectly. Ideally, the king appointed his first-born son as successor to the throne. We know of intrigues over under-age successors from case files, and occasionally it becomes clear that a particularly strong man from outside the royal family took the throne by force. He founded a new dynasty, but always took care that the idea of divine fathering and unbroken continuity was preserved.

Only someone who took over the rituals and the external form of power could become the legitimate ruler. The Ptolemaic kings, originating from Macedonia, had themselves represented on the walls of the temples of Philae and Edfu in traditional pharaonic clothing carrying out the ancient rituals, and even the Roman emperors, whose province Egypt had become, were depicted in the Ancient Egyptian manner.

Myth and Reality

The ruler had to carry out rituals similar to those in the pictures, especially on his accession to the throne. He shot arrows against possible enemies towards all four points of the compass and made a celebratory circuit of a marked-out area symbolising the kingdom. After 30 years, he had to repeat the rituals, and – at least at the beginning of Egyptian history – at the same time demonstrate his physical powers, which were magically renewed by the gods.

The strength of the belief that each pharaoh united and so re-created the kingdom is also shown in the Egyptian calendar. Unlike Christians and Moslems, they had no founders of religion whose birth or death determined the year zero. The Egyptians reset it with every king and started dating from their accession to the throne, for instance, day three in the 2nd month of the Nile inundation, in the 10th year of government of King X.

The history of their country was represented for the Egyptians by a chain of kings, grouped in dynasties. The first known to us, called Narmer or Menes, lived in 3000 B.C., the last, Cleopatra VII, died in 30 B.C. when she lost her country to the Romans. Egypt's history was recorded in the temples. It was not significant events, not wars, catastrophes or conquests that were recorded there, but the names of the kings, the number of years they reigned, when temples were founded, ceremonies and possibly the height of the Nile inundation. The relationship with the gods was important, as they had the power to make the inundation come or stay

King Djoser running around an area symbolising his kingdom thirty years after his ascent to the throne. This ritualistic action demonstrated the physical strength of a king and his constant renewal by the gods.
Relief in the tomb complex of Djoser, 3rd Dynasty

⬚ = house

◁— = large

per-aa = palace/pharaoh

King Merenptah standing before the falcon-headed god Horus, who is carrying the crown of Upper and Lower Egypt for him. It states in the supporting text: Merenptah is praying to Horus, for which Horus is rewarding him.
Painted relief in the tomb of Merenptah, Valley of the Kings, 19th Dynasty

The Depiction of Power

The pharaohs are still very much with us, thanks to the artists and craftsmen who developed the royal picture formulae. The external character of his power included the ruler's attributes: his clothes, insignia and the gods which accompanied him in animal form. The most important of these was Horus, the falcon-god, "whose eyes were the sun and the moon and the tips of whose wings touched the edges of the world." Horus was regarded as son of the gods, as was the pharaoh, and so the king was identified with Horus as "Horus in the palace". The image of the falcon was a reference to the divinity of the king and also to divine protection.

The vulture-goddess Nekhbet from Upper Egypt and the snake-goddess Wadjyt from Lower Egypt were regarded as female protectors of the king. They embodied both parts of the country and jointly defended the ruler. The snake-goddess decorates the royal diadem in the guise of a dangerously rearing cobra.

The insignia of power was the golden flail and crook in the hands of the pharaohs, relicts of early times when the Egyptians still wandered through the desert as nomads. With the whip they drove their herds of cattle, with the crook they caught the animals by the hind leg – the pharaoh acting as supreme shepherd. The animal hide, part of the ceremonial dress of the pharaoh, must also have originated from these legendary early days; "strong bull" was one of his titles. In addition to this, he is usually represented wearing a short pleated kilt made from white linen, and the strengthened head-dress, which was twisted together at the nape of the neck into a bulging plait. For ceremonies, a long, thin (artificial) goatee beard was tied on – even if he, like Hatshepsut, was a woman. The Pharaoh could wear six different crowns, which were the main insignia of his power. Each had its own symbolic value; the two most important were the white crown of Upper Egypt and the red of Lower Egypt, and they were often combined as one of the many signs for the unity of the two parts of the country.

The people only saw their pharaoh in long processions, wearing this ceremonial clothing, which we can still observe today on temple walls. Otherwise he lived cut off in his palace. Within the palace he showed himself ceremonially clothed to the ruling elite at a specially designed "window of appearance", whenever he honoured officials with the "dispensing of rewards". Incidentally, the term "pharaoh" is Egyptian; it comes from the term "per aa", great house, which refers to the royal palace just as much as to the pharaoh himself.

One of the most impressive representations of a tutelary god: Horus as a falcon spreading his wings around the head of the pharaoh Chephren. Perhaps he is not just protecting him, but is one with Chephren – for many years Egyptians in the Old Kingdom believed that kings were personifications of the gods themselves.
Part of a statue, diorite, 4th Dynasty, height 1.68 m, Cairo, Egyptian Museum

The golden diadem of King Tutankhamun with the symbols of Upper and Lower Egypt, the vulture and the royal cobra.
18th Dynasty, Cairo, Egyptian Museum
Lid of one of the four containers in which the internal organs of Tutankhamun were preserved. It shows the head and upper body of the king in full regalia.
18th Dynasty, Cairo, Egyptian Museum

Amenhotep IV, who changed his name to Akhenaten and radically changed the Egyptian divine world. Even representations of this king departed from tradition – his lips are portrayed as thicker, his eyes narrower, his head narrower and elongated at the back and his body rather feminine.
New Kingdom, 18th Dynasty, sandstone, height 64.5 cm, Luxor, Museum for Ancient Egyptian Art

Reproductions of intimate family scenes were also a new departure. Here Akhenaten and his wife Nefertiti are playing with their daughters. Instead of the customary multiple gods, Akhenaten only worshipped Aten, who is visible as the sun-disc, sending his rays with helping hands to the people.
Limestone, height 32.5 cm, width 39 cm, Berlin, Egyptian Museum

Akhenaten, the Revolutionary

We know little more than the names of most of the Egyptian kings, and perhaps the dates they reigned, if they belonged to the Old Kingdom. Not until the 18th Dynasty do we obtain clearer profiles of some of the pharaohs. Among them is Amenhotep IV. He ruled for 17 years, presumably from 1350 B.C. With his protruding lips, slender face, and oversized head, distended at the back, his image diverged dramatically from the standard representation of kings. This king unsettled the country. As supreme priest, he decided that instead of the old multiplicity of gods, only the god Aten should be worshipped, in his guise as the sun-disc. He therefore removed the name of the god Amun from his title and replaced it with Aten, calling himself Akhenaten. Everybody could directly see this one god, they could feel his power. Pictorially, Aten was depicted as a sun-disc, mostly with the uraeus as a sign of power, and with rays ending in hands, which extended the favour of their god to the people. Perhaps the causes of this revolution were not only of a religious nature; it is possible that at the same time the king was depriving the too powerful priesthood of power, wanting to rebuild the administration with which it was closely linked. For he not only built a large temple to Aten in Karnak, but also a new royal capital in middle Egypt. In the 6th year of his reign he left Thebes, the old royal residence, replacing many

officials before the move, and moved to Achetaton, modern-day el-Amarna.

The king altered the style of representation as well as the religion. He clearly distanced himself from the hitherto cultivated ideal by making the back of his head protrude. The somewhat feminine rounded body was also unusual. People have tried to attribute these deviations to deformities or an illness, but there is no proof for this.

Also new in the pictorial repertoire of the pharaohs were glimpses into family life – daughters playing with each other or the royal couple with three of their daughters sitting under the rays of the Aten sun-disc.

After Akhenaten's death – we know neither how he died nor where he was buried – priests and followers of the deposed gods won back their power. His successor Tutankhaten (who had married one of Akhenaten's daughters) changed his name to Tutankhamun, thereby restoring power to the old god Amun, and moved back to Thebes with his royal household. Just as Akhenaten had arranged the destruction of the old gods, his successor, or alternatively the priesthood, persecuted Akhenaten and Aten. The royal capital and the temples he had erected were destroyed or re-dedicated and the pictures of the king were chiselled out. The accusations against him were the most serious that could be made against a king: He had ruled "without Maat", thus against the divine order, and was therefore a "sickness to Egypt". Any remains of Akhenaten and his family were left only by

chance: tomb pictures, reliefs on stones, which were then used as foundations for building new temples, or rubbish from a sculpture's workshop such as the famous head of Nefertiti, which today can be seen in Berlin. The bust is thought to have served as a model, from which other works could be made. This at least would explain why the right eye is a temporary rock crystal. The queen is wearing a wide decorated collar and a blue crown, around which a band is tied. Above her forehead is a rearing uraeus as a sign of royal power, but it has been broken off. As is customary, all that is known of the personality and fate of the queen is that she had several daughters. After the 12th year of Akhenaten's reign she is no longer mentioned, presumably because she died. That her name has become widely known

in the field of Egyptology, and that she is still admired and honoured is due to the accident that this bust remained preserved in the ruins of a sculpture's workshop and – most of all – due to an artist, who transformed Nefertiti's face into a timeless ideal of beauty.

 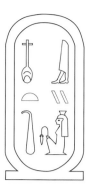

Akhenaten   Nefertiti

Royal names are always
surrounded by a stylised rope,
called a cartouche.

Two of Akhenaten's and Nefertiti's
daughters with extremely elongated
heads at the back. This was one
of the characteristic features in
representations of the royal family.
*Fragment of a wall-painting,
Oxford, Ashmolean Museum*

The most famous bust in Egyptian
art: Nefertiti, wife of Akhenaten,
who has come to symbolise
a timeless ideal of beauty. The bust
came from the ruins of a sculptor's
workshop and may well have served
as a model for further works. For
this reason the stone for the pupil
in the left eye was not needed.
*c. 1340 B. C., limestone,
height 50 cm, Berlin, Egyptian
Museum*

Ramesses II, the Great Master Builder

In contrast to the era of Akhenaten, many of the monuments from the reign of Ramesses II are preserved. There are accounts of his glory hewn on stone, statues, remains of palaces and mortuary temples, the Ramesseum in western Thebes and the rock temples of Abu Simbel. He covered the land from the Delta to Nubia with buildings in a way no king before him had done. He was called Ramesses the Great, he came to the throne around 1279 and reigned for 66 years. He was a master of self-portrayal, of propaganda, not only through buildings, but also in texts. An example: In the famous battle of Kadesh (south of Beirut) he walked into a trap set by the king of the Hittites, his army was beaten and he himself only just escaped death or dishonourable imprisonment. However, on the temple walls at Luxor, the near-catastrophe is made into an act of heroism: "his majesty slaughtered the armed forces of the Hittites in their entirety, their great rulers and all their brothers [...] their infantry and chariot troops fell prostrate, one on top of the other. His majesty killed them [...] and they lay stretched out in front of their horses. But his majesty was alone, nobody accompanied him [...]."

Contrary to all tradition, the war report contains a reprimand. It is addressed to any commander who had given the king false information about the enemy, and presumably served to disempower officers who were anti-peace. For peace was the king's aim. His predecessors had extended Egypt's sphere of influence again, so that it now stretched from the Turkish border far past Nubia. Ramesses wanted to secure the borders, then live in peace having reduced military expenditure. During his reign Egypt flourished for one last time. By glorifying himself with the buildings he commissioned, internal order was also maintained – the king was omnipresent.

We know Ramesses through his self-portrayals, and we also know his body literally from the inside. When it seemed that his mummy was about to disintegrate, it was flown from Cairo to Paris in a rescue operation and scientists used the opportunity to measure and X-ray the royal remains: height: 1.73 m; hair colour: red, grey in old age; age: about 90; arthritis; tooth abscess; hunched back [...].

The mortuary temple of the pharaoh Ramesses II, the so-called Ramesseum, lies opposite Luxor in western Thebes. The tomb is some kilometres away in the Valley of the Kings. The mummy, which came to Europe to be examined, now rests in the Egyptian Museum, Cairo.
New Kingdom, 19th Dynasty

Time and again the entrance to the rock temple of Abu Simbel filled up with desert sand. This photo, taken by Maxime Du Camp in 1850, not only shows us the scale of the expanse of sand but also the size of the royal colossi statues in relation to ordinary people.

To leave a record of his dominion over Nubia, his southern neighbour, Ramesses II had several temples built or cut into the rocks, the most famous of them being the temple of Abu Simbel, which lies north of Aswan. In front of the entrance are four statues of the king, each 20 metres high.

Cleopatra VII, lover of Caesar and Mark Antony and last queen of Egypt, who took her own life. Like Nefertiti, she is immortalised as one of the most beautiful and popular of Egyptian women. Countless dramas, operas, pictures, novels, films and comic strips describe her fate, with more works being added to the list all the time. *Detail from a painting by Artemisia Gentileschi, c. 1640, Rome, private collection*

Cleopatra, the Last Queen

The last pharaoh was a queen who came from a non-Egyptian family. She was Greek. In 332 B.C., when Alexander the Great conquered Egypt, his commander Ptolemy was made governor, and continued to rule in the traditional way as the pharaoh. With Cleopatra VII, the Ptolemaic woman, the history of Egypt as a self-sufficient state came to an end.

Cleopatra was born in 69 B.C. At 17 years of age, she and her brother jointly ascended the throne. Her brother, Ptolemy XIII, was her enemy, forcing her out of Alexandria, after which she joined forces with Caesar, who drove her brother out of the capital. Ptolemy then drowned in the Nile Delta. Caesar, the Roman commander and statesman, had come to Egypt to collect outstanding debts; the fifty-two-year-old and the twenty-one-year-old fell in love and Cleopatra bore him a son, Caesarion.

Caesar had to return to Rome, Cleopatra followed him, she was courted and at the same time reviled as the seducer of the virtuous Roman. When Caesar was assassinated she lost her lover and protector and hurried back to Alexandria. Her father had also been dependent on Rome and she had to choose another Roman to protect her – Octavian or Mark Antony. Octavian the "virtuous", later Caesar Augustus, turned down the queen and her oriental lifestyle. That left Mark Antony, the successful general and ruler of the Roman eastern provinces. In 41 B.C., Cleopatra travelled to Tarsus (on the southern coast of Asia Minor), visiting Mark Antony in a magnificently fitted-out boat, and once again a love story of historic proportions developed.

Naturally, this link was also underpinned by mutual interests – Cleopatra needed protection, Mark Antony the Egyptian reserves of gold and grain, but if we are to believe reports, the couple – she 28, he 42 – were extremely passionate, he following her to Alexandria and she "inventing more and more new forms of sensuality, through which she controlled Mark Antony". Although already married in Rome, Mark Antony married the Egyptian queen, bestowing gifts of large areas of land in the eastern part of the Roman Empire on her and the children they had together. He had a temple built in Alexandria, and obviously lost his predilection for Roman living. In 31 B.C., his old opponent Octavian defeated the Egyptian fleet in a sea battle at Actium and in the following year also defeated Mark Antony's troops. Mark Antony committed suicide. Cleopatra followed suit, supposedly by placing a poisonous snake on her bosom.

Octavian turned Egypt into a Roman province. Cleopatra was 39 years old. It is disputed that she died from a snake bite, but certainly the snake, being both an Egyptian sign of power and a symbol of female powers of seduction, lends her death a mythical splendour. As always, the victors wrote the story and libelled Cleopatra as a "royal whore". But it was just this anti-propaganda that made the queen famous and turned her, a foreigner, into the most popular figure in Egyptian history. Well over 100 plays and operas have been dedicated to her, and films and comic strips ensure that she will not be forgotten by future generations.

Hesyra, one of the highest officials
under King Djoser, holding in his left
hand a staff and sceptre as insignia
of his office. On his back he is
carrying a case for writing brushes
and a small bag for cakes of ink,
on his chest the palettes for the
colours red and black – because all
officials began their career as
a scribe, and writing was considered
the basis of each administration.
*Part of a wooden relief from
the mastaba of Hesyra,
Old Kingdom, 3rd Dynasty,
Cairo, Egyptian Museum*

Servants of the State

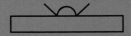

sesch = writing
(palette, water pots, pens and
papyrus scrolls)

Scribes and officials constituted such an important group within Egyptian society that a characteristic postural representation was developed specifically for them. One of these is a person sitting cross-legged with a papyrus scroll on his knees. *Sculpture of the official Ptahshepses from his tomb in Giza, 5th Dynasty, height 32.5 cm, Hildesheim, Pelizaeus-Museum*

A man called Cheti is travelling to the capital with one of his sons, Pepi. They come from far away in the north-eastern corner of Egypt but the father wants Pepi to go to the school for officials, to the "place where you are taught to write". Cheti uses the long journey to explain to Pepi why the latter should take the trouble to learn, "directing his heart towards books". He tells his son that manual workers and craftsmen have a hard life – the barber must seek customers until late in the evening, the bricklayer works bare-chested in the wind, his "arms are constantly in loam, his clothes are covered in it, he eats his bread with unwashed fingers". Scribes on the other hand have an easy time, they are not beaten and fetched for socage, the pharaoh takes care of them and they can make a career as an official.

Copies of Cheti's lessons from the time of the 12th Dynasty were passed down to the 18th or 19th dynasties, obviously being copied time and again in the schools, making a new impression on every generation. It was a type of manifesto for understanding the way scribes and officials saw themselves. Even if Cheti does exaggerate the negative aspects of a craftsman's career, the social distance between them and those with a good knowledge of writing is realistic. "A scribe [...] does not go without," it is said, his scrolls "are a boat on the water".

a papyrus scroll at the end of a word = book, writing, abstraction

A scribe's wooden case with several reeds (hard grasses), which were used as brushes, and the two customary hollows for the black and red scribal ink. *From the tomb of Tutankhamun, New Kingdom, 18th Dynasty, Cairo, Egyptian Museum*

Supporting the State

As well as hieroglyphs and a simpler cursive script, the educational programme included everything that a pharaoh's functionary would need to know, such as places and regions, plants, gods, celebrations and the functions and forms of salutation within the civil service hierarchy. Besides specialist knowledge, the official had to learn the basic principles of the various "wisdom instructions", and he also had to follow them. That is to say, he was taught correct behaviour. Two precepts were considered particularly important: justice towards those weaker than oneself and obedience towards those more senior. This obedience was synonymous with adapting to existing rules and power structures. "Emulate your fathers and forefathers. We can only work successfully by following tradition." On maintaining proper self-control, "Only those who exercise restraint command respect, and a man of character, who is also rich, asserts himself in the administration like a crocodile."

One of the most important tasks of the officials consisted of calculating and distributing the riches of the land, or providing the workers for large undertakings such as building a pyramid. They had to learn to do sums and some exercises have been preserved. For instance: "How do you

An official with a rolled-up measuring rope on his knees. The ram's head with a plumed crown personifies the god Amun, saint of field measurers.
Kneeling figure of Penonuris, from Abydos, New Kingdom, 18th Dynasty, granite, height 43 cm, Cairo, Egyptian Museum

The ancient Egyptians already wedged their writing reeds behind their ears so as to have their writing equipment ready to hand. *Relief from the mastaba of Kaninisut, Giza, 5th Dynasty*

Imhotep was in charge of the work on the first large-scale tomb made of stone in Egyptian history, the Step Pyramid of Djoser (3rd Dynasty). Over the millennia the architect was deified and worshipped by scribes as one of their saints. *Seated statue of Imhotep, Berlin, Egyptian Museum*

distribute 100 loaves of bread between ten men, if three of them – the sailor, the captain and the doorman – are to get double rations each time? You increase the number of people to be supplied to 13; divide 100 by 13; that makes 7 9/13; you say: this is the ration of the seven men, the others receive the double ration."

Of course, the pupils did not always follow their teacher's instructions or the wisdom texts, which they had to copy out. "I have been told that you neglect your writing and indulge in wild pleasures [...] you are in the brothel [...] turning somersaults [...]". Those who did not want to listen, had to feel: "the ear of a boy comes to be on his back, and he listens to his beating".

In the Old Kingdom, individual officials trained their pupils themselves and used them as assistants, but in the Middle Kingdom the practice of teaching them in schools began. The most respected was the prince's school. Here the pharaoh's sons, his family and the highest officials were taught and occasionally also boys who had been especially recommended, perhaps like Pepi. The vizier – highest official and king's deputy – had control. One of them, Imhotep, vizier of Djoser and responsible for his Step Pyramid, was highly respected and later deified. Scribes were in the habit of sprinkling a drop from their water bowl in his honour when starting work.

Bureaucracy

The great significance of letters, numbers and officials in Egypt can be explained by the annual Nile inundation. It flooded the fields and the extent of this inundation had to be put on record and re-measured every year. Bureaucratisation was therefore the necessary consequence of a constantly recurring natural event. There is however another, seemingly more important, reason. At the beginning of Egyptian history, the country and people were regarded as the property of the pharaoh. The farmers had to hand over the harvest to him, he gave the corn to the craftsmen, officials and priests, while those who worked on the land were left with a small portion for growing crops for their own consumption. In the Old Kingdom, Egypt was a centrally organised welfare state, and could not be ruled without officials who were able to write, calculate and keep archives. Of course, that only applied to the leading figures, and as long as the central power remained intact, there was always a flourishing trade in barter at a lower level. The fragments of pottery from the New Kingdom, found in the craftsmen's village of Deir el-Medinah, give us further details (see p. 88) concerning a jug of honey, a donkey and coffin decoration. But the craftsmen received their wages in the form of grain from the administration. There were no coins but copper weights, so-called "deben", which formed clearing units for bartering. A jug of honey was worth one deben, a donkey 31 deben. If the central supply system broke down under a weak pharaoh, the prices rose sky-high and the poor had little to eat. On the whole, though, the price structure remained surprisingly stable over three millennia.

Since the extent of the Nile inundation was uncertain for each coming year, future harvests could not be predicted and stockpiling was necessary. Examinations of mummies show that that was not always successfully achieved – about 30% of the dead had suffered from malnutrition in their youth. The famous Old Testament story of Joseph also revolves around the threat of famine. The Jewish boy, sold into Egypt as a slave, was said to have interpreted a dream for the pharaoh. The king had seen seven fat cows in the dream, which were being eaten by seven thin cows. Joseph interpreted this image in the following way, "seven years of great abundance are coming throughout Egypt, but seven years of famine will follow them. Then all the abundance in Egypt will be forgotten." The pharaoh appointed Joseph, the wise foreigner, as vizier, and the latter stored the excess from the good years. "When the famine had spread over the whole country, Joseph opened up all the grain houses and sold grain to the Egyptians [...] and all the countries came to Egypt, to buy grain from Joseph." The biblical story gives the credit to Joseph, but does not mention the army of Egyptian scribes and officials, without whom the stocks could not have been collected, documented, guarded over a long period of time, controlled and finally distributed. Joseph's relief operation was only able to succeed with the

The officials of a store house taking delivery of storage vessels for oil or wine. The harvest varied considerably according to the height of the Nile inundation, making stockpiling by the state vital.
Wall-painting from the tomb of the official Neferenpet, Thebes No. 178, 19th Dynasty

If a pharaoh wanted to reward an official or officer, he gave him land or property as a fief, or gave him a gift of gold. Here Tutankhamun is presenting the victorious commander Haremhab with several gold chains.
Part of a wall-relief from the tomb of Haremhab in Saqqara, 18th Dynasty, Leiden, Rijksmuseum van Oudheden

aid of a competent central administration and a smoothly running civil service.

The Egyptian kings knew full well how important for themselves and the population the civil service was, and they always took very good care of their elite. "Make your officials rich, and they will implement your laws," one pharaoh advises his son. "Since anyone who is rich in his own household has no need to be partisan," he will also not be so easily bribed. Wealth meant gold and precious stones or owning land, and early on the kings began to reward their higher officials with land. They gave them villages complete with their inhabitants, but reserved the right to demand everything back, if the official should prove to be disloyal. This made the bestowal of the gift both an honour and at the same time a means of discipline, at least under strong pharaohs. Under weak kings it became inheritable family property.

The significance of the scribe-officials is also made clear in art. They and the priests were the only career groups represented by special symbols. On reliefs, they are characterised by their working tools. They are carrying reed pens, water pots and a palette on a string over their shoulder, even if they are at the top of the hierarchical ladder and order the writing to be done rather than doing it themselves. Sculptures show them in two postures; either they are depicted sitting cross-legged, with their writing slate on their knees, or they appear – from the time of the Middle Kingdom – as a cube with a head. That is, the crouching body is stylised as a block with only the head jutting out. These "block statues" symbolise concentrated power and at the same time demonstrate, with their simple geometric form, the need for order to which the officials were committed.

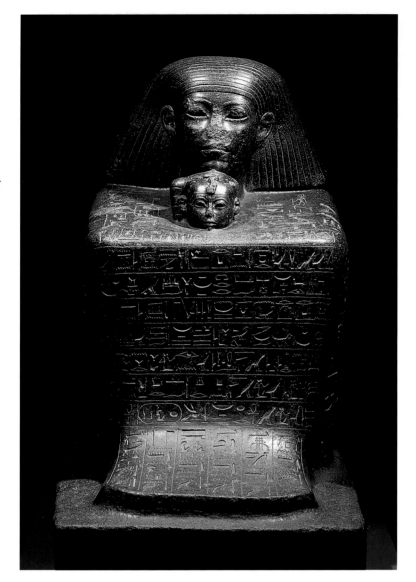

Often the highest officials also brought up the royal children and occasionally they were portrayed together such as Senenmut with Princess Neferura, daughter of Queen Hatshepsut.
New Kingdom, 18th Dynasty, granite, height 100.5 cm, Berlin, Egyptian Museum

An office with scribes and archives from the 5th Dynasty, more than 4,500 years ago …
Panel of a wall-relief from the tomb of the official Ty at Saqqara

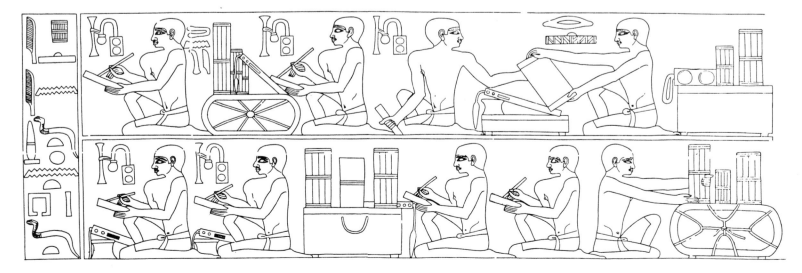

Part-Time Priests

From the New Kingdom onwards, priests can be recognised in representations by their bald heads. After the officials, they were the second most influential group of men and were often identical to the former. There was no separation between church and state: the pharaoh was also the highest priest, the gods looked after the well-being of the country, as taking good care of it was one of the state tasks.

This took the form of constantly repeated rituals, which the priests carried out as representatives of the pharaoh.

It would have had little to do with the idea of a personal calling and religious piety. The pharaoh replaced the highest priests personally and provided the temple with estates, the products of which could be sacrificed to the gods or used to feed the priests. Like the Catholic churches and monasteries in Europe in the Middle Ages, the Egyptian temples were big landowners, making them powerful institutions. Their property could consist of mineral mines, fishing fleets, herds of cattle or beehives. Properties further afield were not normally worked or managed by the temple workers themselves, but leased, the payment of the leases being a fixed percentage of the yields, mostly paid in grain or flax. One papyrus speaks of a fleet of 21 boats belonging to the temple, which sailed up and down the Nile collecting grain and oil from the leaseholders, that is small farmers, and taking it into the temple store cupboards.

The stores were not only used for personal requirements; they formed a royal stockpile which could be stored safely in the temple area, surrounded by high walls. The granary of the Ramesseum at western Thebes, when full, would have been able to feed up to 20,000 people for a whole year. Naturally, these large religious enterprises could not function without scribes, administrators and officials.

Herdsmen drive cattle towards overseers, officials and possibly the owner, who are sitting high up in the shade of a pavilion, in order to get an overall view, presumably for estimating taxes.
From the tomb of Meketra, Thebes No. 280, painted wood, height 55.5 cm, length 173 cm, width 72 cm, Cairo, Egyptian Museum

Clay model of grain silos. The burial object for an unknown person from the Middle Kingdom shows the high rank held by those that managed the stockpiling.
From a tomb in Gebelen, Middle Kingdom, 11th Dynasty, width 21 cm, Turin, Museo Egizio

The way that the religious-state institutions were organised was also economically significant. It seems that only the officials and the highest priests, with their special religious knowledge, were permanently employed. According to notes from the 5th Dynasty the other staff, the many guards, doorkeepers, store workers, and purification priests, only worked every ten months. Their work was organised along the lines of a job-share system and was obviously well remunerated: according to the accounts found, apart from the daily ration of bread, beer and grain, the part-time priests also received meat and clothing. In this way, the temple gave part of its income back to a population group that was ten times as large as the same group of full-time priests would

On the right-hand side is a storehouse with workers and overseers, on the left people waiting who want to collect their wages in kind, for which purpose they have each brought a white bag. There are also people waiting below amongst the trees for a haircut.
Wall-painting from the tomb of Userhet, Thebes No. 56, New Kingdom, 18th Dynasty

Scribe-officials were also needed on the battlefield. One is counting the piled-up hands of enemies killed in action, the other is making notes and adding up.
Relief in the mortuary temple of Ramesses III, Medinet Habu, New Kingdom, 20th Dynasty

wab = a priest

(committed to purity)

Dschehuti = Thoth

To be able to write, the ends of the reeds were cut obliquely at the front and then chewed until they were soft enough to make brushes. Thoth, the tutelary god of scribes, is preparing himself for his duty as clerk of the court at the Court of the Dead.
From the Book of the Dead of Herihor, 21st Dynasty, London, British Museum

A scribe in traditional pose with crossed legs is unrolling a papyrus scroll, his ink palette lying on his left knee. Above him Thoth is sitting on a throne embodied as a baboon with a crescent moon and sun-disc on his head. The small statue clearly shows the religious dimension of writing and administration.
From Amarna, New Kingdom, 18th Dynasty, slate, height 14 cm, Cairo, Egyptian Museum

have been. After their period at the temple, they returned to their villages in order to resume their usual work there.

It has been estimated that only about one per cent of the population could write, keeping the state in order as officials and priests. However, those with a good knowledge of writing had a second very important task – they had to preserve the names and actions of the dead in perpetuity. They had already practised writing biographies as pupils – these were idealised texts which were read out at the Court of the Dead: "I gave bread to the hungry, clothes to the naked, brought those with no boat to shore." These stand- ard formulations were occasionally expanded. The following was proudly recorded on the statue of the vizier Amenhotep, called son of Hapu, in the New Kingdom: "I rose from the young men of my lord (the king), my reed pens organised the counting of millions, and I put them into companies [...] I counted the booty of His Majesty's victories [...] I made the name of the king to be everlasting [...]."

One of the Egyptians' main aims in life was not to be forgotten after death and not only the scribes, but everyone in the land believed that this aim could only be achieved with the help of the written word. So here was another reason, albeit nothing to do with administration, why being able to write was so highly regarded in Egyptian times:

"Portals and houses have been destroyed,
The priests of the dead have vanished,
Their tombstones covered with filth.
Their tombs have been forgotten.
But their names live on through their books,
Which they wrote while they were alive."

Priests could be recognised by their shaven heads; this one was called Ka-aper and was also a high official. As a sign of his rank he is carrying a cane. Since the gods determined the well-being of the land, there was no conflict of interests in serving the state and the temple at the same time.
From the mastaba of Ka-aper at Saqqara, 5th Dynasty, wooden, height 1.10 m, Cairo, Egyptian Museum

It was important to the Egyptians
that hieroglyphs looked beautiful.
This text, which was to lead the
deceased through the underworld,
was inlaid in coloured paste into
cedar wood. It decorated a coffin
from the fourth century B. C.
Detail of an inscription on the
sarcophagus of Djeddjehutiefankh,
from Hermopolis, Turin,
Museo Egizio

The Art of Writing

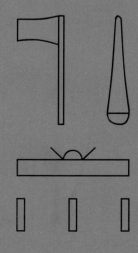

medu netscher = God's words

| | | =

shows plural

Egyptian script was invented around 3000 B.C., when the state came into existence and Upper and Lower Egypt were united.

For a long time the hieroglyphs consisted of approximately 1000 symbols – stylised people, animals, plants, implements etc. This number only increased in the Late Period.

The term "hieroglyph" comes from the Greek (hieros = holy, glyphein = writing). The Egyptians themselves called the hieroglyphs "God's words", attributing their invention to the wisdom-god Thoth, and even had their own goddess of writing, Seshat.

Hieroglyphs were used above all for writing memorials, for chiselling out texts to last for all eternity. Using reeds, the Egyptians wrote on papyrus in a cursive, sketchier form of hieroglyphs. This script is called hieratic. Besides this, in the Late Period, there was an even more fluent script, demotic, which was used for documents and lists.

Although it was called "holy", the script was invented for practical reasons. The organisation of an empire made it necessary to record and preserve facts and to communicate with people in far-flung places.

At first, the Egyptians used pictorial representations, so-called ideograms (the portrayal of an object describing the thing which it represents). Three drawn pots registered a tax contribution to the pharaoh of three pots of oil. For ten

The Egyptians considered that Thoth, the ibis-headed god of wisdom, was the inventor of writing. With the goddess of writing Seshat he is writing the name of King Ramesses II on the leaves of a tree. *Wall-relief in the Ramesseum, the mortuary temple of Ramesses II, Thebes, 19th Dynasty*

Hieroglyphs, chiselled in stone, were certainly meant to last for ever. The signature of Imhotep, the famous vizier and architect, can still be read today on the base of the statue of his king, Djoser. *Old Kingdom, 3rd Dynasty, limestone, Cairo, Egyptian Museum*

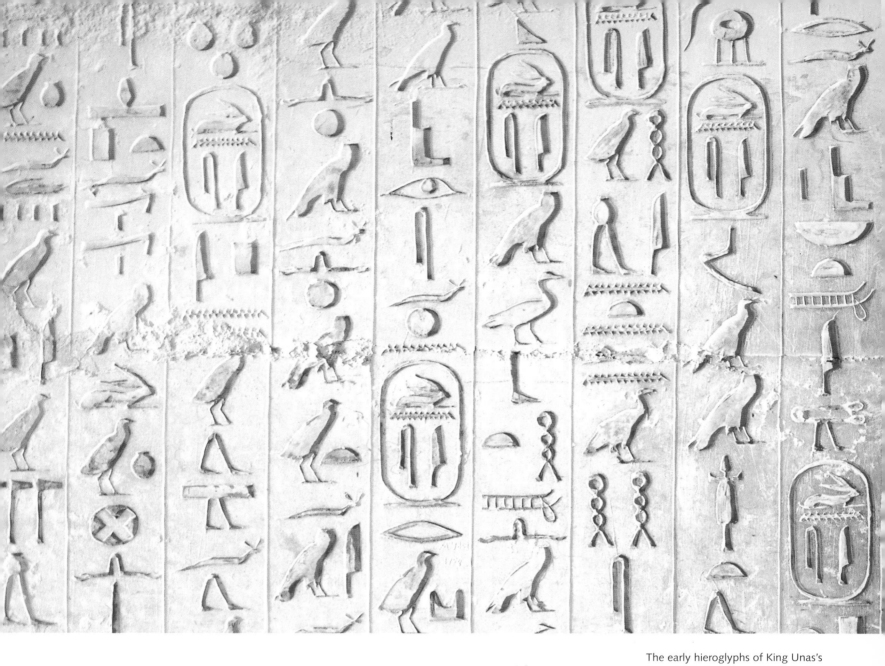

The early hieroglyphs of King Unas's Pyramid Texts were most artistically executed, with blue incorporated in the colour of the sky. Unas was one of the first to decorate his underground burial chamber with spells, which were supposed to help him ascend to heaven.
Saqqara, Old Kingdom, 5th Dynasty

The Egyptians of the New Kingdom painted their texts on papyrus with writing reeds using an elegant cursive script.
Detail from the Book of the Dead of Maiherperi, Thebes, Valley of the Kings, New Kingdom, 18th Dynasty, length 117.5 cm, height 35 cm, Cairo, Egyptian Museum

pots, ten lines could be placed next to a pot; for a thousand, however, this was impractical. The names of those who owed the tax and the pharaoh were also difficult to depict. However, an ingenious invention helped somewhat. To represent the things which were hard to portray, something was drawn which sounded similar, and here it was not the sense of the character, but its sound, which counted.

Since in Egyptian the number 1000 and the lotus plant are both called "Kha", the plant was drawn instead of the number thousand; thus 2000 pots of oil could be represented by a pot and two lotus stems.

The name of one of the first kings "Narmer" was written with a fish (nar) and a chisel (mer).

The mouth was called "ra" in Egyptian; therefore its picture was used for the sound "r". From these types of phonograms (the picture standing for a certain sound) an Egyptian alphabet of 25 "letters" was put together, with which, in principle, every Egyptian word could be written.

3 pots of oil

ear   small boat

2,000 pots of oil

Nar-mer

Egyptian Alphabet

a	w	n	ch	g
b	r	s	t	
i	h	sch	tsch	
p	h		d	
y	f	h	q	
aa	m	ch	k	dsch

Deciphering Hieroglyphs

Unfortunately, the Egyptian scribes were not satisfied with using these 24 phonograms. They placed less value on simplicity or a workable system than on possible variations and visual beauty, and therefore invented more and more symbols with multiple consonants (i. e. symbols corresponding to a combination of letters) in the Late Period. Usually they wrote down the consonants, leaving the vowels out as in Hebrew and Greek. The hieroglyph for mouth can therefore be read not only as "r" but also "ra, re, ri, ro, ar, er, ir" or "or", which means that we do not really know

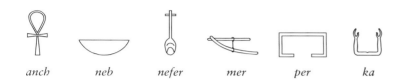

| anch | neb | nefer | mer | per | ka |

how the Egyptian language sounded. So that we can pronounce it, Egyptologists always put an e between the consonants if there is no vowel. As without vowels many words are similar to one another (e. g. in English "band" and "bond"), the scribes put determinatives, signs without phonetic value, behind them, indicating which types of words they were.

Hieroglyphs could be as vivid as any picture. So as not to cause offence, occasionally they were only depicted in a distorted way, for example the male figure belonging to the name of the deceased.
Coffin of Idu, cedarwood with decoration, from Giza, Old Kingdom, late 6th Dynasty, Hildesheim, Pelizaeus-Museum

For instance, two legs for words to do with movement.

A papyrus scroll for abstract concepts.

A man for all male beings,

a female for all female beings

and a man with beard for divine beings.

Deciphering is made more difficult by the fact that words and sentences are separated neither by gaps nor punctuation and the hieroglyphs can be written from right to left, left to right, or top to bottom. The hieroglyphs for animals and people indicate the direction, as they are always facing the beginning of the word.

The juxtaposition of phonograms, determinatives and ideograms, which is where it all began, is confusing. It was this combination, among other things, that made deciphering hieroglyphs impossible for a long time.

Specialist craftsmen built the royal
tombs at Thebes, decorated them
and fitted them out. An elderly
carpenter saws a plank of wood,
another is making a gilded coffin
decoration.
*Tomb of the royal sculptors
Nebamun and Ipuki,
Thebes No. 181, 18th Dynasty*

The Tomb Workers' Strike

pa cher = tomb

 =

at the end of a word indicates that
it is a house or a building

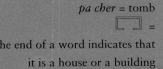

The first strike in world history began on 14th November 1152 B.C. (at least the first which is documented). On that day in the 29th year of the reign of Ramesses III, about 60 workers laid down their tools. Led by the scribe Patwere and two foremen, the stone masons, carpenters and artists closed their places of work in the Valley of the Kings, on the west bank of the Nile in the Egyptian capital Thebes. Instead of decorating the pharaoh's tomb, which they had cut out of the rock, they went over the mountain back to their village, passed through it and marched into the fertile land below. They were heading for the mortuary temple of Ramesses II, the Ramesseum. Situated there was the administration centre, with its well-filled storehouses, from which they received their wages. When they arrived at the temple gate they staged a sit-in. "We are hungry and thirsty", was their complaint. They emphatically demanded the distribution of food, which constituted their wages, now overdue by a month. In vain. They returned the next day. They expressed themselves so emphatically or argued so convincingly that Mentmose, the chief of police in the temple area, personally set out to inform the mayor of Thebes. When he returned in the evening without having achieved anything, the strikers lay down in front of the temple gate once more, determined to pass the night there this time – fortified by 55 small sweet cakes, which the scribe Patwere had brought for them during the course of the day.

Officials are presented here in a dignified way, befitting those who were responsible for order in pharaoh's kingdom.
Statuette with divine standard, 19th Dynasty, wooden, height 27 cm, Turin, Museo Egizio

The protesting tomb workers marching to the temple of Ramesses, because supplies are stored there with which they should have been paid.

In spite of that, in the morning they renewed their complaints at the top of their voices, hunger and thirst driving them on. "We have no clothes, no oil, neither fish nor vegetables. Let the pharaoh, our good master, know; send for our superior, the vizier, so that he makes sure we get food."

The Nile inundation had been favourable, the granary was full and the strikers suspected that a corrupt administrative official was delaying paying their outstanding wages.

For this reason they wanted to turn to the vizier, to whom they directly reported. This threat had an effect. Finally, the temple officials recorded their protest, and handed out the supplies. The workers received their monthly rations of four sacks of grain and one and a half sacks of barley each. They withdrew and resumed work – the three-day strike was finally over.

The Ramesseum, monumental mortuary temple of Ramesses II and important economic centre for the region.

The centre of Thebes was on the site of modern-day Luxor. The necropolis and the workers' village lay on the western bank of the Nile.

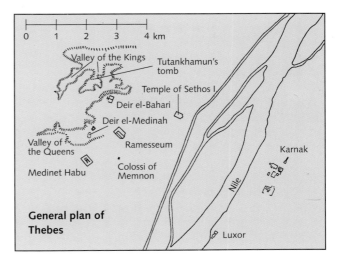

General plan of Thebes

Bearers of Secrets

The workers went on strike several more times in the following, unsettled centuries, which were plagued by civil war. Only a very self-confident group could afford such protest actions. They could not have been driven by real hunger, since the storage cellar in their village provided space for considerable amounts of grain, and they received a generous monthly ration from the state. Most inhabitants of the Nile valley had to make do with less. The workers' strike had much more to do with maintaining their standard of living. The pharaoh's tomb workers formed a privileged elite: master builders, carpenters, stone masons, sculptors, "outline artists" and painters, all masters in their own areas. They were entrusted with the important task of preparing the "House of Eternity" for their kings, thereby ensuring the king's survival. They worked on the west bank in the Theban necropolises, the "Place of Truth", the "Great Square, which sinners may not enter".

There is no proof for the persistent legends that for reasons of confidentiality the king's tomb was built by prisoners, that the pharaoh was buried by night and the entire building team was killed afterwards.

On the contrary; these tomb specialists were always urgently required, for of course after his accession as ruler each pharaoh strove to have his own tomb built as quickly as possible. It had to be finished during his lifetime. Occasionally he was in such a hurry that he appropriated the grave of his predecessor and left him in a modest temporary chamber.

The tomb workers' ghetto lay in an easily guarded desert valley. Excavations revealed streets and outlines of houses in the village with an Arabic name, Deir el-Medinah.

Information on the village inhabitants has been left by the villagers themselves, in the carved rock and fitted-out burial chambers. Here a falcon is spreading its wings protectively over a door, and on the wall the master of the tomb is drinking from a pond.
Tomb of Pashedu, Thebes No. 3, Ramesside Period

bak = working

The Craftsmen's Ghetto

As the tomb workers were bearers of secrets – they knew the location of the king's tomb – they and their families were housed in a narrow, easily overlooked valley. It was a type of ghetto, far from the fertile land, walled with two gates guarded by Nubian police. The workers were only allowed to leave the village to climb a steep path over the mountains, which still exists today, "where the vulture queen, who loves the silence, lives," to go to their place of work. Their protest march to Ramesses' temple broke all the rules and was unheard of. Only since the kings of the 17th Dynasty had migrated to Thebes from Memphis had they had themselves buried in hidden rock tombs in the Valley of the Kings, at the foot of a pyramid-shaped mountain. A village was constructed for the tomb workers, which today is called Deir el-Medinah, Arabic for "town cloister". It existed for around five centuries until the end of the second millennium (c. 1050 B.C.). Generations of specialists lived there and passed down their technical and artistic skills from father to son. Ironically, we know far more about

them than the masters they served, the almighty pharaohs of that time.

Within the walls there must have been about 70 one-storey whitewashed houses with red doors, packed tightly on both sides of a narrow covered path. Around 500 men, women and children lived in them. Usually only the women and children stayed in the village. While the men were working they slept in temporary huts at the tombs. They normally only came into the village on their days off (every ten days) or for the numerous celebrations. Archaeologists have dug out doorposts on which the name of the erstwhile inhabitant can still be read in hieroglyphic script; here lived the craftsman Sennedjem, opposite the scribe Ramose with his family. Not only names but also the faces of some of the village inhabitants are well known to us, for they have drawn portraits of themselves and their neighbours on the walls of burial chambers, which they carved out for themselves in their spare time with the help of colleagues, and skilfully fitted out in the rocks above their village. Several can still be seen today. Of course, they are smaller and less ornate than those of the pharaohs – but often surmounted by a small

The one-storey houses with roof terraces in Deir el-Medinah must have looked similar to this stone model from Graeco-Roman times. *Hanover, Kestner Museum*

A small pyramid often topped the tomb entrance – the old symbol for royal tombs had become common property. *Restored entrance to the tomb of Sennedjem*

Touching portraits of the village inhabitants decorate the walls of the tombs. Sennedjem's small daughter is standing, with a duck and lotus flower, under her mother's chair.
Detail from the tomb of Sennedjem, Thebes No. 1, 19th Dynasty

Sennedjem and his wife Iineferti receiving cold water from their son Bunakhtef, who, dressed in the traditional tiger skin, is acting as mortuary priest for his parents.
Tomb of Sennedjem

pyramid: the old symbol of a royal tomb had become common property.

Almost opposite his house is Master Sennedjem's tomb chapel and on the walls of the small, still intact burial chamber we see the owner himself, his wife Iineferti, his son Bunakhtef, who is bringing sacrifices to his parents, and the couple's younger children, who sit under their seat with their fingers in their mouths. The fact that the craftsman takes his measuring rule into the tomb with him shows how important his job was to him.

Ramose has had himself immortalised as an "honest scribe" in his chapel. He worked in this important role from c. 1275 B.C. for 38 years in the village, a well-off man who had three similar tombs constructed.

He and Mutemwija "the mistress of the house whom he loved" were childless, so they erected stelae, memorial stones in honour of various deities, among which was a large stone phallus. To no avail. Archaeologists today are still in the dark as to whether the nine other women in Ramose's burial chamber were relatives, servants or concubines, as the texts give no information.

The "honest scribe" Ramose is depicted at prayer in bas-relief on the pyramid-shaped gable of his tomb chapel.
Turin, Museum Egizio

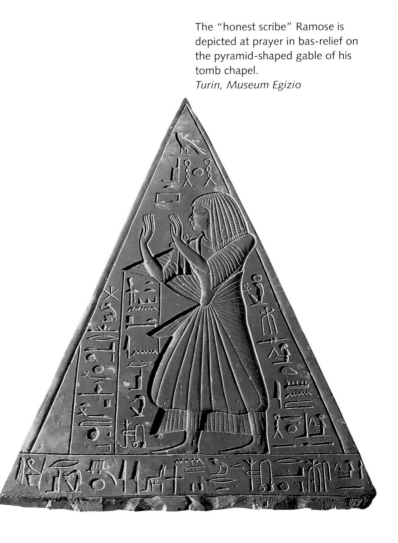

Fragmented Archives

We know all this, because a large part of the village archives have been preserved. Archaeologists found them in a well at the nearby temple of Medinet Habu, where presumably the archive was taken and stored in the insecure times at the end of the 2nd millennium B.C. It consisted of papyri but above all of fragments of clay and slivers of stone, called ostraca. The workers drew up plans and sketches and the scribes wrote their lists on these valuable documents, which now give us a unique, detailed picture of the life of the common man in those days.

It was the job of the scribe and his two assistants to keep a precise diary of all work procedures: for instance, they counted the baskets of building rubble that were carried out of the subterranean passages and recorded how many wicks were handed out each day for the oil lamps to light the work in the dark burial chambers. The lists indicate that the working day was divided into two parts of four hours each with a midday break. Handing out and returning the expensive copper or bronze tools was also controlled. They belonged to the state, the degree of wear and tear was recorded very carefully each time – ten copper pointed chisels were worth about as much as a tomb worker's annual grain ration.

But above all the scribes kept daily records of the presence and absence of the workers. So, for example, we learn that in the 40th year of the reign of Ramesses II a certain Neferabu was missing, because he had to embalm his

A list of dashes – presumably for grave goods, consisting among other things of two daggers and eight divine beards – on an ostracon measuring 13 x 20 cm. This piece of limestone was used as everyday writing material for notes and sketches.
University of Leipzig, Egyptian Museum

The architect Kha from Deir el-Medinah took his work tools with him into his tomb: a gilded folding box and a wooden case for his hand scales.
18th Dynasty, Turin, Museo Egizio

brother, and Hehnektu, because he had to wrap his mother's body. Wadjmose took a day off to build his house and Pendua, because he wanted to go drinking with his friend Khons. Eye problems and scorpion bites are listed several times as reasons for staying away from work. Even brewing beer for holidays was accepted as well as various family celebrations. One craftsman apologised for his absence by saying that his wife had rendered him unfit for work during a marital row.

A carpenter's adze, with bronze blade and wooden handle from the 18th Dynasty, was used to smooth out larger pieces of wood. The heavy wooden mallet from the New Kingdom was a tool used by the tomb workers.
Hildesheim, Pelizaeus-Museum

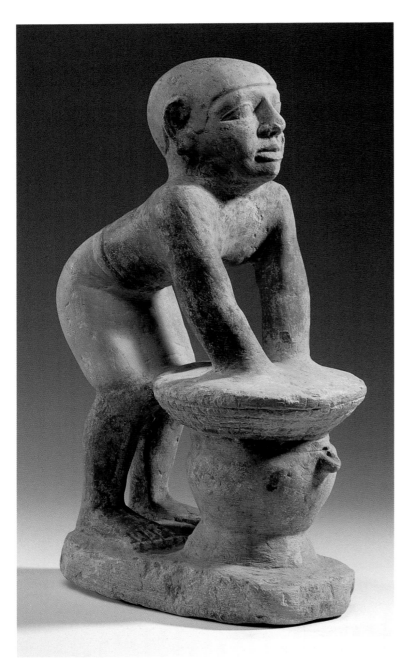

A man brewing beer, at that time a staple food. A worker's household consumed an average of three and a half litres per day.
From Giza, Old Kingdom, limestone, height 16 cm, Hildesheim, Pelizaeus-Museum

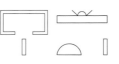

per medjat = library, archive

Unshaven and unkempt, a carpenter
is working with his adze on
scaffolding.
*Fragment of a wall-painting,
provenance unknown,
18th Dynasty, height 15 cm,
Berlin, Egyptian Museum*

The Scribe With Illegible Handwriting

The "honest scribe" Ramose, who drew up many of these lists, had particularly elegant, sweeping handwriting; however, an adopted son and his successor Kenherchepeshef wrote almost illegibly, causing problems for the Egyptologists. In the 33rd year of the reign of Ramesses II (c. 1247 B.C.) he is mentioned for the first time on an ostracon as Ramose's assistant. In the 40th year of his reign he was named as his successor and over the next 40 years recorded the building of no fewer than three royal tombs for the pharaonic administration. He was very old when he died, and already 60 when he married a girl of 12 named Naunachte. He left her the majority of his goods including a papyrus, which today is kept in the British Museum in London. On it the scribe had copied, in his own hand, the hymns, highly topical at the time, praising the victory of Ramesses II at the battle of Kadesh (see page 50).

The back of this papyrus is even more interesting. There we find a text which was already 500 years old in Kenherchepeshef's time and provides an unusual insight into the subconscious of the Ancient Egyptians. It lists 108 dreams, points to them as divine prophecies of the future of the dreamer and offers interpretations. John Romer, an English Egyptologist, has researched the text: profit and loss play a large part in it, equally the threat of food shortages, violent death or maiming. Dreamers could avoid their catastrophes, it says, if they ate fresh bread and herbs soaked in beer on awakening and at the same time said a certain magic spell.

The stone headrest on which the scribe with such illegible writing laid his head at night has survived, with his name on it, and is decorated with prayers and pictures of mythical creatures to protect his dreams. There is also an amulet, which was to keep headaches at bay. On the other hand, Kenherchepeshef's tomb has so far not been discovered. This scribe does not seem to have been a very likeable person; he was involved in two cases of corruption and forced the workers to help him during official work-time, while still treating them badly. "I am like a donkey to you. If you have beer, you can't be bothered with me," complains the artist Parahotep, "but if there's work to do, you send for me […]." Kenherchepeshef was obviously a powerful, self-confident official: Above a shady stone seat near the tomb of the pharaoh Merenptah he has personally and for all time carved into the stone "The seat of the scribe Kenherchepeshef".

Fragment of manuscript showing a hymn on the victory of the pharaoh Ramesses II in the battle of Kadesh, written by the scribe Kenherchepeshef in his almost illegible handwriting.
London, British Museum

sesch = scribe

The crocodile was feared and worshipped as the god of fertility and water. Crocodiles played a role in magic practices and were, like other holy animals, also mummified.
Roman Period, length 37.5 cm, Cairo, Egyptian Museum

Taken from the dream book of the scribe Kenherchepeshef

If you see a person in the dream:
– an old man digging
    = good: that means prosperity
– drinking warm beer
    =bad: that means sorrow
– eating crocodile meat
    = good: he will become an official
– looking in the mirror
    = bad: a new woman
– dead
    = good: that means a long life

Magic spell, to prevent bad dreams from coming true:
"Come to me, come to my mother Isis;
See, I perceive things that are far from my city"
(at the same time you should eat fresh bread and green herbs soaked in beer).

Magic spell against the evil spirit causing headaches, who feeds on excrement and lives on dung heaps:
"Back, Shehakek, you who come from the heavens and the earth […] Nedrachse is the name of your mother, Dshubest the name of your father. If he attacks the scribe Kenherchepeshef, son of Sentnefer, I will call on […]."

(after Morris Bierbrier: The Tomb Builders of the Pharaohs, London 1982. John Romer: Sie schufen die Königsgräber, die Geschichte einer altägyptischen Arbeitersiedlung, Munich 1986)

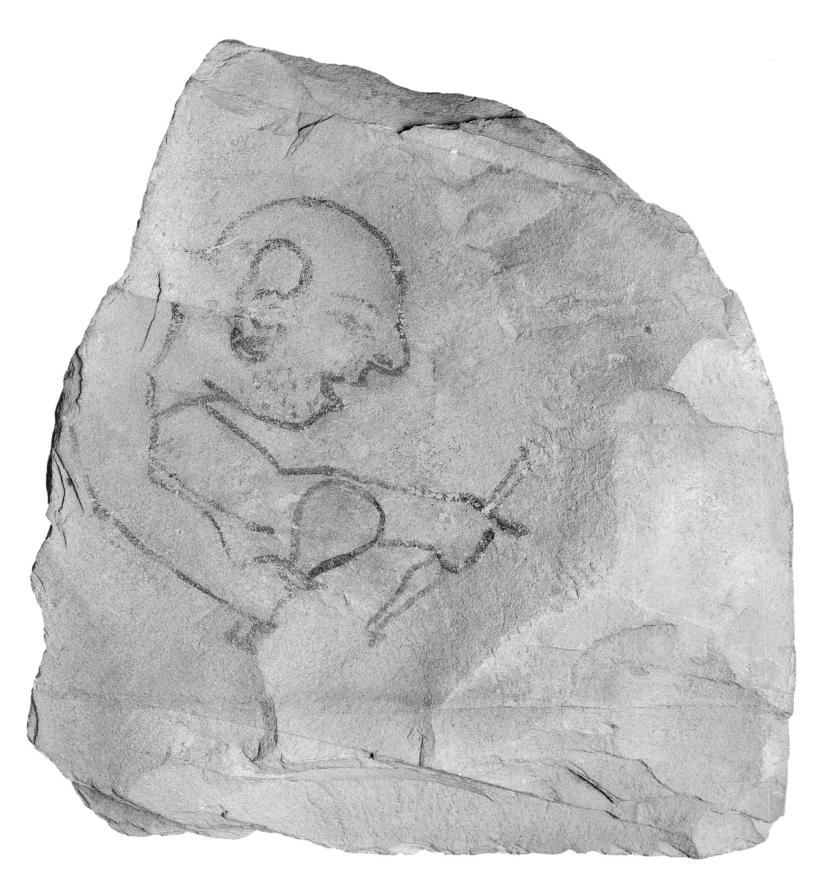

The sketches on the ostraca were brutally realistic – in contrast to the idealised representations destined for eternity in tombs and temples. *Stone mason on a limestone fragment, Ramesside Period, 14.5 cm x 13.5 cm, Cambridge, Fitzwilliam Museum*

Paneb

Paneb, the Thug

Also well known to Egyptologists is a certain Paneb, who provided excitement in the village towards the end of the 19th Dynasty: a competent stonemason and foreman, but at the same time a thug, drunkard and womaniser. At least, that is what his enemy, the craftsman Amennachte maintains, in a long indictment drawn on a papyrus. He accuses Paneb of taking the position of foreman, to which he (Amennachte) was entitled by law, and of behaving in an ungrateful way to his adoptive father; he "picked up a stone and smashed down Neferhotep's door." The violent Paneb "hit nine men tonight" and threatened his colleague, the foreman Hay: "I will come upon you in the desert and kill you." Hay survived, however, and Paneb turned to other pleasures. "He carried on with Tuju," reports Mannachte, outraged, "when she was married to the workman Kenna, with Hurro […] and then he even indecently assaulted her daughter." "He ripped Iymuai's (the wife of the complainant) clothes off, threw her on a wall and raped her."
All this does not seem to have done Paneb much harm. He was greatly feared as a thug and had protectors in the administration, and he must have bribed the scribe Kenherchepeshef several times. However, the situation changed when Paneb was convicted of having taken part in a tomb robbery. He was thought to have stolen a wooden goose from the burial chamber of King Merenptah and a bed and stones from a private tomb to use for his own tomb. By doing this the foreman had contravened the oath "to alter no stone in the surroundings of the pharaoh's tomb", which he, like all his colleagues, had to take. But worse still: he supposedly sat drunk on the sarcophagus of the pharaoh – which was both treason and sacrilege. This time it came to court, the judgement is unknown, but presumably Paneb was convicted and sentenced to death by the vizier. In any case, his name disappears from the reports and he was replaced as foreman. The customary way for a tomb robber to die was by impaling.

Clearly erotic representations like these are seldom seen in Egyptian art. Egyptologists believe they are connected with fertility rites.
Late Period, painted limestone, 16.5 x 17 x 9.5 cm, New York, The Brooklyn Museum, Gift in memory of Dr Hirsch and Charles Edwin Wilbour Fund 58.13

A baker baking bread. He is shielding himself from the heat with his hand. Each day the workers received roughly ten kilos of wheat, which made roughly five kilos of bread, sufficient to feed a household of six. *Statuette from Giza, Old Kingdom, height 26.2 cm, Hildesheim, Pelizaeus-Museum*

ta = bread

ḥeb = celebration

Erotic scenes from the so-called Turin Papyrus. It dates from the Ramesside Period and was found near Deir el-Medinah. *Re-drawn and completed from a fragment in poor condition, Turin, Museo Egizio*

Bread and Bartering

For lesser criminal and civil cases the village inhabitants formed a court for themselves. Those involved were their own prosecution and defence, and it seems that they had a certain amount of fun with splendid prolonged trials. The best known dispute from Deir el-Medinah dragged on for 18 years. In it, two particularly dogged opponents argued over a pot of lard. The worker Menna had sold it to the chief of police Mentmose on credit (the same Mentmose who was active on behalf of the strikers). He had faithfully promised "I will pay for it in barley", but did not. The plaintiff Menna won this trial and also another – against the water carrier Tsha, who had sold him a sick donkey. Most trials were about material goods, and through them we know some prices. There were no coins but instead standards for comparison, by which the value of an article could be measured: for instance the sack of wheat (76.56 litres) or the copper deben (91 grams). Sandals cost between a half and three deben, depending on the model; three to five deben was paid for a shirt and five deben for a pig; a loaf of bread cost only a fifth of a deben, while a coffin cost twenty-five deben. The tomb workers were paid for their work directly by the state, which collected the produce directly from the farmers as taxes. With an average monthly ration of four

Painted storage vessel with original top from the tomb of the architect Kha. *Height 38 cm, Turin, Museo Egizio*

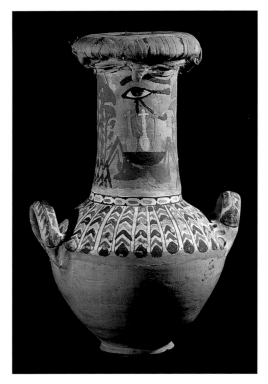

sacks of emmer-wheat, a craftsman had at his disposal ten litres of wheat each day, making about five kilos of bread, enough for a household of six people or more. With the one and a half sacks of barley he could brew about 115 litres of beer per month, that's three and a half nutritious litres per day.

The village lists show that every ten days two fishermen delivered fresh or dried fish to the value of 200 deben each. A water carrier supplied the village well, which lay in a desert valley, daily with water from the Nile, and on special occasions the pharaoh sent "rewards": "Oh workers, well-chosen, skilled and strong [...] your provision will be bountiful and you will not go short," one of the kings promised them" [...] for I know what truly arduous work you do, and how you can only rejoice in your work if your belly is full!" The "rewards" consisted of salt, natron, which was used as soap, wine, dates, sweet cakes and ox meat from the nearby temples and pots of white cheese.

What they did not need for themselves the tomb workers bartered for other goods; as efficient carpenters and artists they could make or paint sumptuous coffins in their spare time. They did well and celebrated in great style. Whenever they had the opportunity they held parties, for example in honour of the founder of the village and patron King Amenhotep I. "The workforce celebrated in his honour for four days," according to one report, "full of drink and with their wives and children." If we are to believe the largely destroyed "erotic papyrus" of Turin that was found at Deir el-Medinah, its inhabitants were no strangers to sexual excesses. Presumably there was some sort of brothel in the village and the violent Paneb would not have been the only one to have lost his inhibitions during the drinking sessions which lasted several days.

In the Valley of the Kings

There were particularly extensive celebrations in the village when the king died, because this always meant prompt initial payment for the workers and – if the new pharaoh was in a particular hurry, because he was already old when he ascended to the throne – generous bonuses. Scarcely had the dead pharaoh been buried, when a special commission headed by the vizier appeared in the Valley of the Kings at the "Great Square", to search for a suitable place for the site of the new tomb. That became increasingly difficult, for in the course of 420 years 62 tombs had been constructed (only five remained unplundered), and it became increasingly common for workers to come across a forgotten chamber or an old passage. Once a suitable place had been found, the master builder submitted the plan, usually in accordance with a seldom varied lay-out: a steep, long passage leading down to the chambers; a shaft would have impeded access and collected rainwater.

Next, the workers got down to work. In the first building phase, lasting about four years, the rock was cut away with wooden hammers and copper chisels and the building rubble carried outside in baskets. Then the walls were smoothed, cracks filled in with clay and plaster and the entire area coated with a thin layer of stucco as a base for the wall decorations. This dragged on for many years; most kings' tombs were unfinished when the king died and remained so. The work continued all year round, the workers being organised into two teams, one for the left and one for the right side. But owing to the confined conditions there were never more than about 120 men being used – no comparison with the masses of people used to build the pyramids. The Egyptians did not differentiate between workers and artists. As a team they created the innumerable square metres of painted relief scenes, which decorated all walls from the entrance to the burial chamber. The artists sketched the outlines and wrote the spells, before the stonemasons

The Valley of the Kings, the workplace of the tomb specialists, lay within walking distance of their village. The workers stayed in temporary accommodation there.

set-maat = Valley of the Kings, actually: place of truth, the Maat, symbolised by a feather

To enable the dead king to ascend straight to heaven, the vaulting above his sarcophagus represented the night sky complete with constellations. The bull on the right corresponds to our Great Bear, the other constellations remain a mystery.
Astronomical ceiling. Detail from the tomb of Seti I

The tomb of pharaoh Seti I is a masterpiece of the craftsmen of Deir el-Medinah from the 19th Dynasty, completely decorated in painted raised relief and well maintained.
Valley of the Kings, Thebes No. 17

Carpenter manufacturing gilded coffin decorations. *Tomb of Nebamum and Ipuki. Thebes No. 181, 18th Dynasty*

Plan of the tomb of Ramesses IX. This drawing on an ostracon was probably used as an orientation plan for the overseer supervising the building site. *20th Dynasty, Cairo, Egyptian Museum*

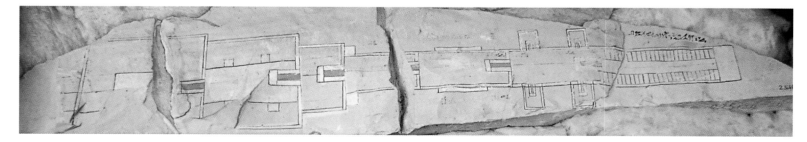

executed them as raised or sunken relief. Finally, the painters provided painted figures and hieroglyphs – all completely in accordance with a predetermined formalised aesthetic.

The pleasures of this life, which the workers, priests and officials wanted to take into their tombs, are missing in the case of the kings; only the mythical journey of the dead pharaoh by night in the barque of the sun god is ever depicted.

It travels through the underworld, in spite of its dangers, re-emerging safely every morning into the light.

The workers learned not only the techniques of representation from their fathers, but also the secret spells, which could "prompt" the painted subject into new life. Only then were the pictures imbued with magic power. This was also true of their own tombs. The artist Neferhotep, adoptive father of the wild Paneb, reported "I opened the eyes of the coffin for Ramses the gatekeeper". That means, the coffin, which he made for his gatekeeper colleague, became a living part of the body of the deceased. With the eyes painted by Neferhotep, the dead man could see.

The tomb workers of Deir el-Medinah served their kings for the very last time at the beginning of the last millennium B. C. Most of the pharaohs' tombs which had been built and decorated so artistically were broken into and plundered during the civil wars under Ramesses XI (c. 1098–1069 B. C.), and the inhabitants of the village took refuge in the secured temple of Medinet Habu. When order was restored, the priests and the workers who had escaped gathered the stolen mummies and hid them in two secret chambers, the "cachettes", where they were discovered in the 19th century. The kings of the 21st Dynasty transferred their capital from Thebes to Tanis in the Delta where they were buried. The community of tomb workers from Deir el-Medinah dispersed – they were no longer needed.

The daughter-in-law of Sennedjem, named Isis, had a coffin in his tomb. On the lid is a youthful portrait of the woman dressed in white. In her hands she is holding tendrils of ivy.
Wood with painted stucco coating, Cairo, Egyptian Museum

This close-up clarifies some of
the working procedures: on one part
of the stucco base the outlines have
been drawn, gone over with bright
paint and only then finished in
reddish-brown face paint.
*Wall-painting in the tomb of
Nefertari, Great Royal Wife of
Ramesses II, 19th Dynasty, Valley
of the Queens, Thebes*

Egyptian Art

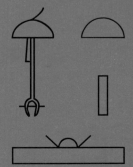

hemut = art, craft
(on the left, a drill)

As in a comic strip, different plots can be depicted next to each other and one on top of the other. Top right, grapes are being harvested, then trampled by foot. Bottom right depicts fishing and poultry-plucking. The size of the people corresponds to their importance: the tomb owners are larger than their servants, who in turn are larger than the workers.
Tomb of the official Nakht, Thebes No. 52, 18th Dynasty, New York, The Metropolitan Museum of Art, Rogers Fund, 1915 (15.5.19e)

In the preliminary drawings a network of auxiliary lines ensured that people and objects were depicted in proportion and accurately to scale. As work progressed, they were hidden by the paint.
Unfinished wall-painting in the tomb of Senenmut, Deir el-Bahari, Thebes, 18th Dynasty

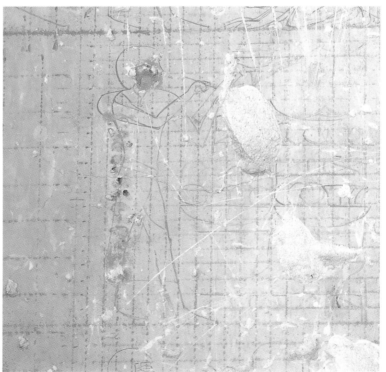

Egyptian artists understood how to create a harmonious human form using two different dimensions (head, mouth, torso and legs in profile, eyes, upper body and hands shown from the front).
Tomb relief of Ashaket, Thebes, Middle Kingdom, Cairo, Egyptian Museum

Art without Perspective

Egyptian painting and reliefs have no **perspective**. The three-dimensional is missing, with people, animals and objects arranged in two dimensions next to and above one another. Everything is shown in outline and representations in profile are preferred. However, the side view is often combined with the front view: for people, for example, head, mouth, torso, legs and feet are shown in profile, while eyes, upper body and hands are shown from the front. A pictogram emerges, which should arrange the clearly recognisable information.

Even the **colour** has a particular significance – reddish-brown for the male body, yellow for the female, while Osiris the god of death is black or green.

The differing sizes of the people indicates their importance: the pharaoh appears bigger than the official, the master of the tomb bigger than his servant.

A **system of baselines** subdivides the wall to be decorated, so that defined areas emerge, which are to be covered with various scenes. Within this so-called "register", as in our cartoon strips, plots can be depicted next to and above each other.

A further network of auxiliary lines (which will not be visible later) ensures that people and objects are depicted in **proportion** and accurately to scale. These divide the register into squares of equal size, into which the figures are fitted in accordance with stipulated standards: a standing person, for example, accounts for 18 squares from the baseline to the hairline, one sitting, for 14 squares. This "canon of proportion" makes it possible, by halving or quartering the squares, to create smaller but always well-proportioned figures.

Statues were also made according to this system. The linear network of the canon of proportion was drawn on all four sides of the stone block and renewed again and again during the course of the work. Statues were to be looked at from the front; they show people in positions of repose, and a majestic step to the front is the biggest movement.

An influential Egyptian invention was the **block statue**. Wrapped in his coat, the scribe or the high official crouches like a block, with only the head jutting out – an immobile, concentrated bundle of strength and power.

It was not a good likeness that was striven for in the portrait of Queen Tiye, mother of Akhenaten, but rather a timeless ideal of beauty in accordance with the stipulated canon of proportion.
Relief fragment, Thebes,
18th Dynasty, height 35.5 cm,
Berlin, Egyptian Museum

Artists in the modern sense did not exist. There was no question of being original or creative; we have only found that in sketches on fragments of clay and stone. The craftsmen/artists were judged on their ability to reproduce the picture programmes, which were handed down, in harmonious compositions in accordance with "holy" pattern books: "I know […] how to calculate correctly […] so that a body is put in its correct place," boasts the artist Iritisen from the Middle Kingdom. "I understand how to make a male figure step forward and how to position a female figure, or a captured bird." Art was produced as a team effort and was not signed.

The same standards determined Egyptian art for over 3000 years, ensuring its clarity and abstraction, which we find so "modern" today. Only when the chaos broke out and state order broke down in the "Intermediate Periods", did the grid structure and canon of proportion disappear. The representations became more awkward, harmony and order faded away.

Order and symmetry determine the construction of the picture – only at first sight do the three pairs of geese appear to be painted true to life; in reality they are strongly stylised.
Wall-painting from a tomb at Meidum, Old Kingdom, 4th Dynasty, Cairo, Egyptian Museum

Each time political order in Egypt broke down the artistic canon also lost its way – the proportions were no longer true. The stele of Mentuhotep from the "Intermediate Period" between the Middle and New Kingdoms documents this loss of harmony in the times of chaos.
Roughly carved limestone slab, Berlin, Egyptian Museum

The name and title of a person was considered to be as much a part of the individual as their soul and shadow. They could not be missing from any representation in the tomb or temple.
The scribe Hesyra, from Saqqara, Old Kingdom, 3rd Dynasty, wooden, height 114 cm, Cairo, Egyptian Museum

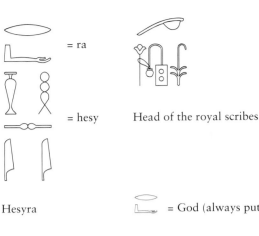

= ra

= hesy

Head of the royal scribes

Hesyra

= God (always put first)

Art as Magic

Palaces and dwelling places were built from bricks of Nile mud; these have vanished and with them all private wall decorations. The Egyptian works of art which have been preserved nearly all come from temples and tombs. They were made for the gods or the dead, not for art-loving on-lookers. Only the statues in front of the temples and the reliefs on the external walls of the pylons, which also served as political propaganda, were intended for the public. Statues or wall pictures representing the dead in the tomb had a definite purpose. Eternal life was only ensured if the souls could return to their bodies at any time. Hence the costly mummification. Statues or likenesses were regarded as replacement bodies in the event that the mummy was destroyed and could be brought to life through magic, which the dead had recourse to.

These works of art therefore served as material aids for eternal life, as magic utensils. They did not have to be realistic, as the outer body was idealised for the underworld: age and illness were omitted, women always appeared young and beautiful, and men imposing and in their prime.

Of course, to identify the deceased, their name had to appear on the statue or likeness. The name was regarded as part of the personality – without it there was no individuality and no magical revival.

For the Egyptians, the entire universe was full of magic forces and naturally this played a major part in creating works of art. When craftsmen were working, they recited magic formulae, which – together with their expert skills – were passed down from father to son. And on the finished work they carried out the ritual of the Opening of the Mouth, through which at the time of burial the mummy was "revived" for the underworld. "I am the master of the secret," boasted the artist Iritisen, whom we have already mentioned, "I have practised every sort of magic". In this way, the pictures "lived" for the Egyptians, as long as they were created in accordance with the correct standards.

The pharaoh is eternally smiting the captured enemy, the block statue can stand up in its place in the museum at any time and "go out into the day".

One of the most impressive inventions of Egyptian art is the block statue – reducing people to a concentrated bundle of strength, ready to stand up when they hear their name.
Statue of Amenemhet, 18th Dynasty, granite, height 80 cm, Cairo, Egyptian Museum

This wooden statue of a woman
dates from the Old Kingdom, the
time of the pyramids. Her face has
been just as artistically composed as
that of Egyptian men. Did she also
have equal rights when she was
alive?
From Saqqara, 4th Dynasty,
height 61 cm, Cairo,
Egyptian Museum

Free Women
in Pharaoh's Land?

set = woman

⌒ = t

is the hieroglyph
for the feminine ending

In Egypt, "the women attend market and are employed in trade, while men stay at home and do the weaving", the Greek Herodotus comments. Disconcerted by certain customs in the country on the Nile, he occasionally made false generalisations. In his homeland, women belonged in the home, leaving business to the men. In Rome and in most societies in the Ancient World it was exactly the same. Females were considered incapable of thinking for themselves throughout their lives, and came under the guardianship of a male relative. He had to represent them in court and they could take charge neither of themselves nor their property.

Court records provide us with evidence to the contrary: The Egyptian woman in the New Kingdom could act on her own behalf in court and bring actions, even against her own father; she was regarded as an independent legal entity. She could dispose of her wealth herself. "I am a free woman in Pharaoh's country," declares a certain Naunachte from the craftsmen's village of Deir el-Medinah in her will. "I have raised eight children, [...] but now I am old and they do not look after me. To those of them who have stood by me, I will leave my property." Naunachte disinherits some of her children and bequeaths a valuable bronze vessel to her favourite son.

It is undisputed that Egyptian women enjoyed more legal rights than was customary in other societies. However, Egyptian laws were not codified and it is questionable, with this lack of an organised legal system, how much use women were able to make of their rights. Egyptologists argue about this, one speaking of "equal status and equal value" in Ancient Egypt, another considering this to be pure fiction.

Female servants were depicted as young, nude and charming. They were supposed to look after their master in the underworld, just as they had in life.
Statuette from Thebes, New Kingdom, gilded wood, height 13.8 cm, Berlin, Egyptian Museum

A girl fanning the fire in the oven, presumably a slave, as were most of the female servants in the New Kingdom. If she was pretty and healthy, she could cost twice as much as a man.
Ostracon made of fired clay, 20th Dynasty, height 13 cm, University of Leipzig, Egyptian Museum

A woman is sitting in the shade of
a tree, her child tied to her breast.
She belongs to the mass of the rural
population about whom we know
virtually nothing.
*Wall-painting from the tomb
of Menna, Thebes No. 69,
18th Dynasty*

For the majority of women, the question must remain
unanswered. A painting in the tomb of Menna shows
a young woman from the countryside, a child tied to her
breast, who has brought her husband a meal in a basket
while he is working in the fields. However, we know nothing
about her life and status, although farmers' wives made up
over 90 per cent of the female population.

Scarcely any more has been discovered about the many
female servants who helped well-to-do housewives, fanning
the fire in the oven, and serving when guests came for
a meal. They were almost always depicted as young, nude
and charming. In the New Kingdom, they were mostly
slaves, who had to make do with half a sack of grain per
month in Deir el-Medinah.

A housewife in the workers' village paid a trader a good
price for a young Syrian slave, called Gemeni Herimentet
(which means "I found you in the West"): six bronze plates,
ten deben of copper, 15 linen garments, a veil, a blanket and
a pot of honey. That was twice as much as for a male slave –
in the papyrus verifying the deal there was no mention of
any special talents and charms the girl might have had which
would have raised the price.

Fair and Fashionable

We know a little more about women from the numerically small upper class, but whereas their husbands, the scribes and officials, had their dates of birth, career stages, successes and good deeds engraved on their tomb stelae as idealised biographies, the women were not so honoured. They had no opportunity to distinguish themselves professionally, as female scribes or officials did not exist.

The art of writing – so exceedingly important to the Egyptians – was not taught to girls, so far as we know. It is possible that women from the ruling house were an exception, but there is no evidence of this. We cannot say with certainty that any single document handed down was written by a woman and no women are depicted anywhere as scribes at work. In this way, women were condemned to political insignificance; they could only exercise power over men indirectly. It's true they were allowed to inherit and dispose of wealth; however the vast majority were dependent on their husbands to provide for them and so were only self-sufficient to a limited degree. We know next to nothing about the status of women living alone. Widows must often have had difficult lives – otherwise so many men would not have boasted about having helped them.

Nevertheless, wives and daughters of high officials had positions in the Old Kingdom as priestesses of Hathor, later described as "singers of Amun". Serving in a musical capacity in the temple gave them the opportunity to assume noble positions, though there were never any female "lector priests".

Since they didn't write, there are no "wisdom instructions" by or for women; their thoughts or ideals are not recorded on any papyrus, and even recipes have not been handed down. No doubt, as pictures show, they used their reed pens mostly

If women are using a brush in pictures, it is for applying their make-up. They were not taught to write, and were thus excluded from a career in the "scribal hierarchy". They could only exert influence through men.
Papyrus, 20th Dynasty, Turin, Museo Egizio

neferet = the beautiful one

= hieroglyph for "good, beautiful" (heart and windpipe)

Left: the most beautiful of the queens, Nefertiti.
Restored statuette, from a sculptor's workshop in Tell el-Amarna, 18th Dynasty, height 41 cm, Berlin, Egyptian Museum

The Lady Nefertaibet from the Old Kingdom is wearing a narrow, asymmetric leopard-skin dress, which leaves a shoulder and one arm free – a simple and refined fashion.

Relief from a stele, Giza, 4th Dynasty, height 36 cm, Paris, Musée du Louvre

for putting on make-up. When depicted on tombs, they all appear young and beautiful – perfect, which was how they wanted to enter eternity. Fitting the Egyptian ideal of beauty, they had light skin (contrasting with the dark red-brown of the men), and were dainty, graceful, long-limbed, narrow-hipped, with small, high breasts and a relatively large head, emphasised further by the massive wig. This ideal at its most spectacular is embodied in Queen Nefertiti; the "approaching beauty" still enchants all who see her.

Clothing was simple and refined at the same time, made from white linen, which became increasingly fine and transparent through the centuries, and ever more lavishly gathered and pleated. In the Old Kingdom women wore a narrow, figure-hugging, ankle-length slip with straps; in the Middle and at the start of the New Kingdoms the garment came up to just under the bust, leaving the breasts free. Later, fashion dictated a pleated outer garment, which emphasised rather than covered up the body's curves – a flattering, seductive fashion. Added to it were thrifty colourful accessories such as belts, jewellery and net shawls made from pearls. Lady Nefertaibet was striking in her dress made from a leopard skin.

In the New Kingdom too, simple transparent garments emphasise the graceful figures of young servant girls. Obviously the Egyptians enjoyed the sight of beautiful bodies and did not want to do without them in the underworld.
From the tomb of Rekhmira, Thebes No. 100, 18th Dynasty

The queens of the New Kingdom are lavishly dressed: Ankhesenamun, depicted in front of her husband Tutankhamun, is wearing a pleated and gathered outer garment and expensive accessories: collar, belt and bows with the plumed crown on top of her tightly curled wig.
Marquetry with gold, silver and semi-precious stones on Tutankhamun's throne, 18th Dynasty, Cairo, Egyptian Museum

The girl picking flax is wearing her hair in thin plaits, a very common hairstyle among female servants.
Tomb of Nakht, Thebes No. 52, 18th Dynasty

Men and women both wore a lot of jewellery: Princess Khnemet's necklace with amulets, goddesses from both parts of the country, cobra, female vulture and *wadjet*-eye.
From Dahshur, 12th Dynasty, gold, lapis lazuli, cornelian, turquoise, height of the figures 18 cm, Cairo, Egyptian Museum

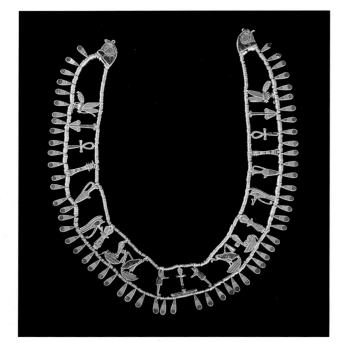

The hairstyle was particularly important; depending on fashion it was long and straggly, curly, ruffled or artistically plaited into small braids and decorated with ribbons and flowers. In pictures, it is hard to decide whether the women have their own hair or are wearing a wig. Certainly for official occasions, upper class ladies seem to have always worn a black wig over their own hair, which was kept short or even shaved off. A shaven-headed woman of the Mereruka plays the harp on her husband's bed. Of course, the wigs, kept in special boxes, were taken into the tomb.

The hair was one of the most important female attractions. How exceptionally seductive it could be is shown by the fact that there were magic potions to make the curls of a rival fall out: "[…] cook a worm in oil and treat the head of the one you hate with it!" In a poem from the New Kingdom a young man says that the loved one "ensnares me with her hair". Even wigs clearly had a strongly erotic charisma for many Egyptians: "He found me alone," said the heroine of a fairy-tale about her lover, "he said, come let us spend an hour together. Let's go to bed, put on your wig!"

A lady getting ready, assisted by two small slave girls. One is bringing a lotus blossom and a necklace that looks like a garland of flowers. The other is adjusting a lock of hair on the wig. All are wearing fragrant incense cones on their heads.
Tomb of Djeserkaraseneb, Thebes No. 38, 18th Dynasty

Artistic wigs adorned the heads of upper-class ladies. The role played by hair and wigs in erotica has been passed down through poems and fairy tales.
Relief, sculptor's model, Vienna, Kunsthistorisches Museum

This anonymous couple from the Old Kingdom demonstrates who was in charge in an Egyptian marriage. Even though the feet are missing we can see that the man is striding forward, and the woman is standing with her feet together. This traditional representational pose typifies the relationship of the sexes to one another.
Old Kingdom, acacia wood, height 69.9 cm, Paris, Musée du Louvre

Uhemka was "a scribe in the filing administration" and overseer of a prince's household. His wife Hetepibes is following him and lovingly places her hand on his shoulder – this is another oft-recurring gesture.
Detail of a relief from the funerary chapel of Uhemka, Giza, Old Kingdom, early 5th Dynasty, Hildesheim, Pelizaeus-Museum

A "Field for her Lord"

In law women may have had equal rights, but in the preserved texts, always written by men, they are portrayed as
stupid and unpredictable creatures. In the Wisdom Instructions of Ani, a woman is described as "very deep water,
whose current is not known". And the sage Ptahotep advises
husbands: "fill her belly and clothe her back [...] for she is a
field, good for her lord [...] You shall not pass judgement on
her, remove her from power and restrain her!"
On one stele from the Late Period it is written that a certain
Taimhotep, married for 14 years, with four children and just
30 years old, died. This is the only summary of the life of a
woman who was not a member of the Royal Family which
is given in any detail, and it was certainly typical: at 12–15

years of age girls were married to a somewhat older man,
apparently with no ceremony or formality. "I took a bundle
of notes to Payan's house," reports a young man, "and I
married his daughter." The marriage was based on nothing
more than an agreement between the bridegroom and the
girl's father, who went to great pains to find her a good
husband.
The married woman is described as "mistress of the household", and that was her life. She looked after the children
and the household, carried out tasks such as weaving,
baking bread and brewing beer, or supervised the servants.
In the tombs, however, the housewife never appears as
"mistress of the house" supervising her household, that is
always taken care of by the master of the tomb personally.
Of course, the life of an Egyptian woman was not strictly

confined to the home. She went to market, and could even sell the products of her labours such as vegetables or cloth, but her most important domestic duty was taking care of the family. Above all, she had to bear children, as "a man to whom no children have been born is like one who has not existed. His name will not be remembered." Of course, a son was vital. Many pregnancies followed, one after the other, and the children were breast-fed for three years. Mortality among mothers and children was high, despite the competence of the doctors and gynaecologists, who were famous far beyond their own country. Besides all kinds of magic tricks, they knew effective methods of maintaining female fertility and for early diagnosis and prevention of pregnancies.

The dwarf Seneb held high honorary offices and supervised the royal wardrobe. In front of him are his two children, next to him his wife, the lady-in-waiting Senetites, depicted with the typical loving embrace. A portrait of a happy family.
Statue group from Giza, mastaba of Seneb, Old Kingdom, 4th or 5th Dynasty, height 34 cm, Cairo, Egyptian Museum

A housewife knuckling down to her work. She appears strong and happy. Her home and family were her kingdom.
Female beer brewer from the tomb of Meresankh, Giza, Old Kingdom, 5th Dynasty, Cairo, Egyptian Museum

hemet = wife

= source, vagina

The first wifely duty in all strata of society – to bear your husband children and look after them, like this farmer's wife, who is carrying her baby in a sling.
Relief from the tomb of Montuemhat, Thebes No. 34, 25th/26th Dynasty, limestone, height 23.9 cm, New York, The Brooklyn Museum, Charles Edwin Wilbour Fund 48.74

Method of telling whether or not a woman will bear a child: *"Put barley and wheat in two sacks, the woman should water them daily with her urine. At the same time, put dates and sand in two other sacks. If the barley and wheat both germinate, she will bear a child. If the barley germinates first, it will be a boy; if it is the wheat, it will be a girl. If neither germinate, she will not bear a child."*

Method of prevention: *"To prevent a woman falling pregnant for one, two, three years: crush acacia tips, coloquintida and dates in half a litre of honey. Impregnate a tampon with it and place in the vagina."*

(quoted after Christiane Desroches-Noblecourt: La femme au temps des Pharaos, Paris 1986)

Egyptian Divorce

If the marriage was without issue, the husband could take a concubine to ensure offspring. That was perfectly permissible but not the rule, except at court (Ramesses II had over 85 children by an unknown number of women). Or he could divorce the infertile woman. That was relatively simple for a man, but expensive. Since marriage was based on nothing more than an agreement (with no legal or religious protection), it could be informally dissolved. A woman from Deir el-Medinah was disowned after 20 years, because she was blind. "I have been blind for 20 years, why did you not divorce me before?" she asks, and takes him to court. We do not know whether she was successful.

If she had borne children and no blame was attached to her, the woman was entitled to be provided for. She had a right to a third of the accumulated increase in value of property during the marriage and of course to the dowry she brought into the marriage. Preserved marriage contracts from the New Kingdom show that cautious fathers tried to safeguard the financial requirements of their daughters in advance. Proof that women also wanted to get divorced exists from 500 B.C. onwards.

Wives also laid claims for provision 'on the other side': they could, at least theoretically, expect professional mummification and a place in their husband's tomb. On many wall paintings and tomb stelae, the wife is sitting on one side of the offering table and enjoying the gifts that ensure survival, although according to examinations of tombs from the Old Kingdom, situated on the west side of the Nile at Memphis, we find that was not the rule. Of the 807 tombs inspected, only 68 belonged to women, and those almost exclusively wives and daughters of kings. In more than half the remaining tombs owned by men, there was no sign or

The master of the tomb, Sennefer, mayor of Thebes, sits large and imposing at the table. Much smaller, his wife Mereti, is at his feet, tenderly embracing his leg instead of his shoulder.
Tomb of Sennefer, mayor of Thebes and administrator of the Amun temple gardens under King Amenhotep II, Thebes No. 96, 18th Dynasty

Careworn and with pendulous breasts, not young and pretty, the woman is at her work. Figures like this are rare, where the reality of old age and the true position of women in Egyptian society is shown rather than the idealised tomb representations.
Old Kingdom, limestone, height 16.8 cm, Paris, Musée du Louvre

mention of their wife. This meant that the worst of all fates, that of the forgotten ones, the true death, had befallen them. In other epochs, wives may not have been so strongly neglected, but even the Egyptian who took care of his wife did not always grant her the place at his side in the tomb. His mother is often sitting there, with the wife on the other hand in small format crouching down at the feet of the extremely important tomb owner, humbly clasping his knee. Whom he took into eternity with him was determined by whoever had control of the financial means of building the tomb. He could even deny his wife her place posthumously. That is verified by the statue of a Mr Sennefer, "deputy governor of the palace" in the Old Kingdom, who sits alone on a bench too wide for him. All that is left of the person who had obviously been sitting next to him is an arm around his waist. It must have belonged to Sennefer's wife. He has scratched out her name and had her image removed, as far as possible.

What women requested from the goddess Hathor is written on a statue from Deir el-Bahari: "Happiness and a good husband". The stability of marriages was supported by the Egyptian sense of harmony, compromise and family. Most men wanted a home with numerous children and a loving wife. "Appreciate the value of your wife," states one of Any's wisdom instructions, "joy reigns, when your

Record of a divorce – the master of the tomb Sennefer is sitting alone on a bench. He has had the female statue which sat next to him removed, only a hand on his shoulder remains.
Mastaba of Sennefer, Giza, Old Kingdom, limestone, height 31.8 cm, Hildesheim, Pelizaeus-Museum

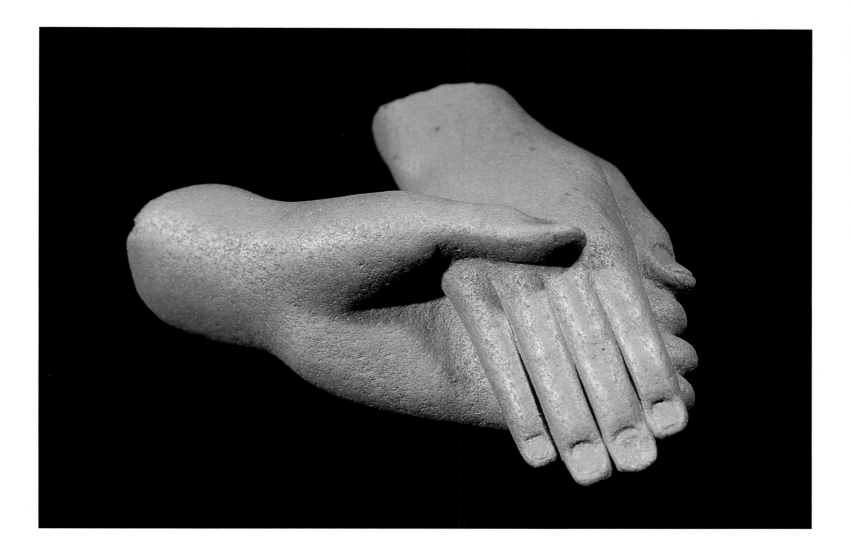

hand is united with hers!" This ideal is recorded in many pictures and statues. The woman is standing with her feet together, close to her husband who is striding out. He is radiating activity and energy, she a sense of peace and security; often she has discreetly placed her arm tenderly round his shoulders. He does not embrace her, but is occasionally holding her hand.

This fragment of a lost statue group consists of two hands showing loving care and marital togetherness. They probably belonged to King Akhenaten and Nefertiti, depictions of whom exhibited more emotion than was usual.
From Tell el-Amarna, 18th Dynasty, sandstone, height 9 cm, Berlin, Egyptian Museum

nebet-per = mistress of the house

Women Pursuing Power

There were very few women who did not follow their husband, but proceeded alone just as self-confidently as he did. There are members of the Royal Household or high priestesses, for example the Lady Imeretnebes from the Middle Kingdom. She bore the title "Revered by the God Amun, God's Wife and Hand of Amun" and had the responsible task of encouraging the deity's fertility by masturbation, and so looked after the country's fertility. In the New Kingdom "God's Wife" held an important role. She had huge estates in Thebes at her disposal, where the priests of Amun had set up a divine state and ruled autocratically. She was usually a daughter of the pharaoh, who resided in the far Delta, but it is not clear how far her power extended. The wife and mother of the king looked majestic wearing the vulture's head-dress, but they were only defined through him, depended on his favour and could exert only indirect influence. The "Great Wife" of Amenhotep III was called Tiye and her portrait bust shows character and a strong will. Tiye's son Akhenaten, the religious revolutionary, gave far more prominence than was usual to his wife Nefertiti and had her – like a king – depicted as a charioteer, engaging in battle. Ramesses II built his favourite wife Nefertari a temple

As self-confident as a man, Lady Imeretnebes is striding forward. She was a High Priestess of Amun. *Wooden statue from Thebes, Middle Kingdom, 12th Dynasty, height 48 cm, Leiden, Rijksmuseum van Oudheden*

Tiye exerted influence as the "Great Royal Wife" of Amenophis III and the mother of Akhenaten. This portrait shows unusually indi-vidualistic features of an ageing, strong-willed woman. Her plumed crown has been lost. *Yew, 18th Dynasty, height 5 cm, Berlin, Egyptian Museum*

of her own in Abu Simbel and a particularly richly decorated tomb.

However, neither Nefertiti nor Nefertari were the only wives of their kings; they suddenly disappeared from the scene and were immediately replaced by another wife, in the case of Akhenaten by his and Nefertiti's own daughter. All three pharaohs mentioned here married their own daughters and there is no proof that these marriages were not consummated or were concluded only for dynastic reasons. In any case, the consummation of the marriages between royal siblings in the New Kingdom has been verified.

Ramesses II had a huge harem, but only his principal wife Nefertari had her own temple, built for her in Abu Simbel. She appears majestic in her tomb.
Wall-painting from the tomb of Nefertari in the Valley of the Queens, Thebes, 19th Dynasty

Nefertiti appears in the foreground at her husband Akhenaten's side more often than other queens. Unfinished heads from a sculptor's workshop in Tell el-Amarna immortalised her as the ideal of feminine beauty.
18th Dynasty, quartzite, height 35.5 cm, Cairo, Egyptian Museum

Hatshepsut, the Woman who Reigned as a Man

There were two exceptional women, Hatshepsut and Cleopatra VII. But whereas Cleopatra as pharaoh carried on the traditional role of the subordinate woman, of the woman who can only wield power over men, Hatshepsut reigned like a man – "twenty one years and nine months", noted the Egyptian historian Manetho, and we can take his calculation as correct.

If Hatshepsut had been born male, the power would have been handed to her on a plate, because she was a princess, the only "legitimate" daughter of Tuthmosis I, second pharaoh of the 18th Dynasty, and his "Great Royal Wife". However, women in Egypt were excluded from the succession to the throne and Hatshepsut was married, as was the custom, to her half-brother, a son of the king and a concubine, who then ascended the throne as Tuthmosis II. After his early death, his eight-year-old son, again by a concubine, was named successor. Hatshepsut herself had only borne him a daughter, Neferura. Hatshepsut should have taken over as regent for this half-nephew, but instead of staying in the background, like other female Egyptian regents, and ceding power when he came of age, she pushed him aside. In 1490 B. C., in the seventh year of Tuthmosis III's nominal

hemef = His Majesty

Depicted as a man, Queen Hatshepsut is offering the god Amun a water jug. At one time this statue looked out from the terrace of her mortuary temple in Deir el-Bahari into the desert valley, but it was found in a nearby marl quarry.
From Thebes, 18th Dynasty, red granite, height 75 cm, Berlin, Egyptian Museum

reign, she proclaimed herself ruler. Pharaoh Hatshepsut proclaimed: "I myself am a God. That which happens, is meant. Nothing I say is erroneous."

Her coup d'état was supported by important administrative officials at court, who were engaged in a power struggle against the military. The army had achieved great influence under Hatshepsut's father, through their victory over the Hyksos, the enemy occupying northern Egypt. The military wanted to fight on, favouring a policy of conquest; the officials on the other hand pleaded to stay within the traditional borders. Hatshepsut sided with the officials and demanded that the destroyed country be rebuilt. When, after Hatshepsut had ruled alone for about twenty years, another enemy, the Mitanni people, threatened Egypt, Tuthmosis III, who had been pushed aside (but not assassinated), made himself head of the army, demanding sole power. The queen disappeared, possibly killed.

Her tomb in the Valley of the Kings remained empty, and her mummy was never found. Her successor obliterated the name of Hatshepsut from stelae and temple walls, defaced her features, and destroyed or renamed the statues. He did not do this because he hated Hatshepsut, but because in Egypt a female pharaoh did not fit in with the "natural" world order.

This fragment of a divine statue with a royal beard also shows the autocrat's attractive female features, well-known from other representations. This too stood on the terrace of her mortuary temple.
Head of Hatshepsut, Deir el-Bahari, limestone, height 61 cm, Cairo, Egyptian Museum

ren = name

She was to be forgotten: Hatshepsut's successors had her name and likeness chiselled away. The water of life given to her by the gods Thoth and Horus did not succeed in immortalising her.
Relief in the sanctuary of Hatshepsut in Karnak, 18th Dynasty

What remains of her

From the moment she seized power, Hatshepsut had herself depicted in an emphatically masculine form, with a naked male upper torso, short kilt and royal beard. However, all the statues show female features, a tapering face, slightly full lips, and almond-shaped eyes. The attractive face of the ruler served as a model for the sculptors of her kingdom, most statues of the epoch looking like her. The queen influenced formative style, just as Akhenaten did later, and used art as a means of power to emphasise her claim to the throne and her legitimacy.

A succession of (unfortunately badly preserved) reliefs demonstrates how Amun himself came to resemble Hatshepsut's mother, the Great Royal Wife, bearing her features. The queen could be distinguished from the god only by his fragrance of incense, which soon pervaded her body too. Sexual relations were discreetly hinted at with both of them sitting next to each other on a bed. Further reliefs celebrate the ruler's great deeds: manufacturing, transporting and setting up two obelisks at Karnak (one is still standing, the other lying there) or a reconnaissance and trade expedition, which in the eighth year ventured to far-away Punt, because Amun longed for his favourite fragrance from the far-off country. This was a land on the African shore of the Red Sea, perhaps in present-day Eritrea. From there, incense trees were brought in tubs, kept damp on the way and probably planted in front of the temples of Deir el-Bahari.

Today, we can see the queen's importance and power most of all in her "House of a Million Years". This mortuary temple of Deir el-Bahari in western Thebes is dedicated to the gods Amun, Hathor and Anubis. In a wide rock basin facing east, surrounded by an impressive sand and stone desert, it stands, half set into the mountain. The central axis of Hatshepsut's temple is aligned with the temple of Amun at Karnak, an ideal straight line leading through the mountain directly to her tomb in the Valley of the Kings. But above all it stands as an immense demonstration of Hatshepsut's own might. With the triumphal avenue of sphinxes – imitated by

Hatshepsut's successors could not destroy her mortuary temple situated in barren wasteland at Deir el-Bahari, Thebes: A very strongly "male" memorial to a female pharaoh.

Senenmut was the queen's master builder, minister and probably also her lover. This portrait sketch was found in his tomb, which he was permitted to build under the queen's mortuary temple.
Ostracon from Deir el-Bahari, height 9.5 cm, New York, Metropolitan Museum

Senenmut is shown here with Hatshepsut's only daughter. We only know the year of his death from the date recorded on the wine jugs in his tomb. For thousands of years the powerful man and his queen disappeared from the memory of the people.
Statue of Senenmut with Neferura, black granite, height 60 cm, Cairo, Egyptian Museum

many successors – the temple made an ideal setting for the ceremonies of a female ruler stressing her legitimacy. Almost immediately after her takeover, Hatshepsut began building. Her master builder was called Senenmut, and he left many hidden traces of himself in the temples: portraits, statues and inscriptions with his name. Senenmut was an efficient overseer, devoted to the queen and probably her lover. As a special sign of her favour, he was given permission to have a secret tomb built under the temple of Deir el-Bahari. But for a thousand years fate separated the servant from his mistress, their names were removed, their facial features chiselled out, and they were not to be able to see, hear, smell, breathe or speak, even in death. For more than

three centuries this "damnatio memoriae", condemning to oblivion, remained in effect. Not until our century did Egyptologists re-discover the identity of the queen and her loyal overseer.

The Pleasures of the Heart

Sechemech-ib = pleasure of the heart

ib = heart =

So that the deceased would not go without good food, even in the underworld, pictures of fruit, vegetables, poultry and ox legs are piled up in front of them. Under the sacrificial table stand amphorae of wine – cooled by green leaves from climbing plants.
From the tomb of Nebamun, Thebes No. 90, 18th Dynasty, British Museum, London

One of the burial chambers of Sennefer – mayor of Thebes during the 18th Dynasty – resembles a wine bower. The ceiling is painted all over with brown tendrils, olive-coloured leaves and almost black ripe grapes. This elaborately stylised but harmonious pictorial effect, creating the atmosphere of a shady bower, fills the observer with cheer.

The walls of other tombs are decorated with hunting scenes or celebrations, fruit and vegetables, poultry and ox legs piled high on tables – the houses of death tell of the joys of life. Certainly they show the burial rituals of the gods, but beside the religious images they also record what the deceased loved in life and wanted to continue to enjoy in the underworld.

A lot of space was devoted to sensual pleasures. Perhaps the Egyptians had even more time to devote to these than other peoples, for the river oasis was – when the inundation irrigated the fields properly – extremely fertile, and there were relatively few wars, as they had no aggressive neighbours. Asceticism and the voluntary mortification of the flesh, as practised in the Egyptian desert by later Christian settlers, was unknown to the Ancient Egyptians. The pictures in the tombs of the officials, priests and craftsmen and some papyrus texts show how much they enjoyed the pleasures of life.

A colourful wine bower on the ceiling of the tomb is a reminder of joyful celebrations in shady bowers and fills the observer with cheer.
Ceiling-painting in the tomb of Sennefer, Thebes No. 96, 18th Dynasty

Sweet-smelling flowers and oils were offered at banquets in the hot climate. The servant girl of the master Djehuti is pouring perfume over a guest's hands.
Tomb of Djehuti, Thebes No. 45, 18th Dynasty

The Lord of the Nose

It seems that for the Egyptians enjoyment came above all through the nose, so much so that a nose hieroglyph was used in every word meaning "pleasure" or "to be pleased". Even the proximity of the gods announced itself by a heavenly scent, called "perspiration of the gods". The Egyptians received the breath of life from the gods through the nose, symbolised by an *ankh*. Incense and myrrh were constantly burnt in the temple to the glory of the gods; "heaven and earth shall overflow with incense," ordered the god Amun to the queen Hatshepsut, whereupon she mounted an expedition to collect incense trees. There was even a god who was chiefly responsible for perfume: Nefertem, the "lord of the nose", who was depicted with a lotus blossom on his head. In all representations of Egyptian banquets, this flower decorates the tables and heads of the guests, so its scent must have been extremely popular. Perhaps while enjoying the scent it was not forgotten that the lotus is a symbol of resurrection, for it blooms with the sunrise, closes at night, then opens again in the morning. We assume that the sense

Mrs Kha's cosmetic box contains various fragrant oils, kept in expensive corked bottles. These refined mixtures, which were particularly long lasting, were an Egyptian export much sought after abroad.
From the tomb of the architect Kha, Thebes No. 8, 18th Dynasty, Turin, Museo Egizio

An artistically carved incense spoon, with a duck-shaped bowl presented by a naked female swimmer. Both female swimmers and water fowl were considered erotic symbols.
From the Fayum, 18th/19th Dynasty, wooden, partly painted, with inlay work, Cairo, Egyptian Museum

of smell was more finely-tuned in man's earlier stages of development than today and it is possible that the Egyptians could also smell more intensely and differentiate more subtly. The Greeks regarded them as experts in perfume, both for refined mixtures and for long-lasting properties. Those "which last the longest are the Egyptian ones", reported Theophrastus (c. 372–287 B.C.), the Greek philosopher. A perfume maker reported that he had had Egyptian perfume in his shop for eight years […] "and that it is still in good condition, actually even better than fresh perfume". The fragrances were fixed in unguents and oils, and packaged in artistically shaped unguent pots and vessels. Distilling in alcohol was still unknown. In the "anointing kitchens" of some temple complexes there are hieroglyphs on the walls recording recipes for perfume but so far it has not been possible to identify the ingredients.

reschut = pleasure   = Nose, fragance, pleasure

Pleasant smells played such a large role that there was a god responsible for perfumes and incenses, called "Lord of the Nose". He wore a fragrant lotus blossom on his head.

Tomb of Horemheb, Valley of the Kings, Thebes, 18th Dynasty

Incense and Unguent

Due to the dry desert climate, unguents and fats were essential for looking after skin and hair, and using them was a basic necessity, like eating and drinking. They were, for example, part of the wages in the workers' village of Deir el-Medinah. The poor used castor oil, the rich used fragrant oils which took up to six months to manufacture. Seven types of unguent, "holy oils", were particularly famous, with names like "festive fragrance" or "Syrian balsam" or even "best Libyan cedar oil".

Fragrant unguents were important for both health and sensory pleasure – the wise Ptahhotep (c. 1300 B.C.) advises the husband to not only provide his wife with food and clothing, but also with unguents: "as a healing aid for the limbs […] with it her heart will be happy all her life."

"Fresh incense under the arms" was said to be an effective deodorant. For festive meals, men and women put aromatic unguent cones on their hair, a solid sweet-smelling oil, that melted onto the hair or wig making it shine and at the same time spreading a pleasant scent. "It would make me happy,"

At the banquet the guests are wearing aromatic incense cones in their hair. These melted slowly in the heat, distributing a pleasant scent, giving the lavish hairstyle gloss and holding it in place. *Unfinished painting from the tomb of Neferronpet, Thebes No. 43*

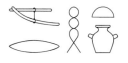

merehet = ointment

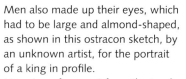

Men also made up their eyes, which had to be large and almond-shaped, as shown in this ostracon sketch, by an unknown artist, for the portrait of a king in profile.
Limestone fragment from the tomb of Ramesses VI, Valley of the Kings, 20th Dynasty, Cairo, Egyptian Museum

The unguents and oils kept in highly imaginative bowls were not only used for beautification. They were essential for skin care in the dry desert climate.
Make-up holder made of ivory, 18th Dynasty, length 13 cm, Turin, Museo Egizio

enthused a young man in the service of his loved one, "to wash the unguents out of her transparent garment."

Men and women both made up their eyes heavily, large and almond-shaped and with changing colours: green in the Old Kingdom, black in the New Kingdom and different shades according to the season. The statues of the gods in the temples were also made up. We can tell from the Nile hymn how important eye make-up was, as it expressly mentions that in times of need "neither eye make-up nor unguent" could be obtained. Looking after their bodies seems for many to have been not only an act of hygiene but also of pleasure. By the 2nd Dynasty, members of the upper classes had bathrooms with showers and mirrors. After eating, bowls of water were brought to them for cleaning their hands. Pride in their own already highly developed culture was sometimes allowed as pleasure. For the Egyptians, all other peoples were "wretches"; they thought they could only live well in their own country. This is also mentioned in the report of an Egyptian official at the end of the Middle Kingdom. He was called Sinuhe and had to flee Egypt, but after years abroad could return. How happy

he was with his bathroom mirror and "exquisite perfumes".
"My body felt years younger, I was shaved, my hair was
combed, I was dressed in fine linen, I was anointed with
fine oils […]."

The name and title of the owner are
inscribed on this razor blade:
"Confidant and chamberlain of
the king, Merireseneb".
*Old Kingdom, 6th Dynasty, copper,
8 x 3.5 cm, Berlin, Egyptian
Museum*

Miniature reproduction of a pot
used for hand washing with a bowl.
*From the tomb of Queen
Hetepheres, Giza, Old Kingdom,
4th Dynasty, gold, height 5.2 cm,
Cairo, Egyptian Museum*

Personal hygiene was of a particularly high standard: the Egyptian
upper class had bathrooms with
shower units at their disposal and
conveniences such as this
"lavatory chair".
*From the tomb of Kha in Deir
el-Medinah, Thebes No. 8,
18th Dynasty, Turin, Museo Egizio*

Wine was mostly produced in bowers in the Nile Delta. The vintners poured it into carefully labelled clay jugs giving the year of the vintage, and shipped it along the Nile throughout the whole kingdom. *Painting in the tomb of Khaemwaset, Thebes No. 261, 18th Dynasty*

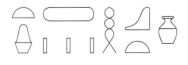

ta henket = bread, beer

Bread and Beer

The national drink of the Egyptians was a thick beer, which with bread made up the basis of their food. Since it did not keep, beer had to be freshly brewed continually in all households. Ground grain was dampened and lightly baked in cakes, then crushed in large tubs and fermented and finally pushed through a sieve. Hops were unknown.

Those who could afford luxuries drank wine, which was cultivated in bower-like constructions on the flat land, mostly in the Delta area. The Egyptians liked it sweet, "sweeter than honey". In a text from the 19th or 20th Dynasty we read of a man who boarded a ship in the town of Ramesses (on the Delta) with 1500 sealed jars of wine and 100 jars of different liqueurs. We can draw the conclusion that there was a lively wine trade. Discoveries from the tomb of the pharaoh Tutankhamun show how high standards were in the upper classes: 26 wine jars stating the vintage, place of origin and name of the wine grower. For

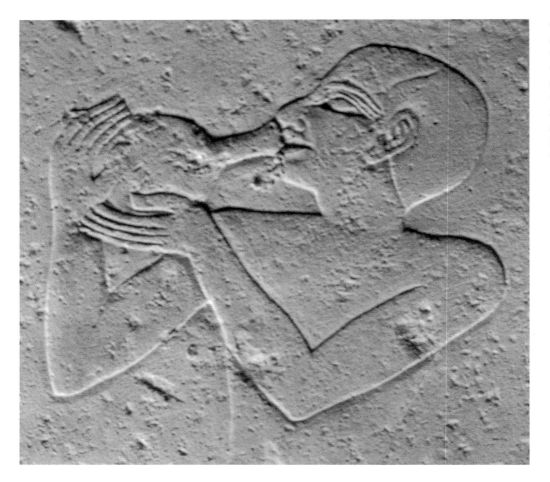

Ordinary workers could seldom afford wine. While they were working in the fields they drank water from a clay bottle, but their everyday drink was the thick, nutritious beer.
Relief from the mastaba of Hetepherachti, Old Kingdom, 5th Dynasty, Leiden, Rijksmuseum van Oudheden

Egypt was a "gift of the Nile" and the river also made a gift to the Egyptians of fish, which they ate far more often than meat.
Detail from a painting in the tomb of Menna – "agricultural scribe" of Tuthmosis III, Thebes No. 69, 18th Dynasty

Very little food has survived over the millennia. These loaves came from the tomb of the architect Kha.
From the tomb of Kha, Thebes No. 8, 18th Dynasty, Turin, Museo Egizio

example, it said "year four (of Tutankhamun's reign, thus 1329 B.C.), sweet wine from the house (temple estate) of Aten – may he live and stay hale and hearty! – from the western bank, master wine grower Apereshop". The contents of the jugs have unfortunately completely dried up. What the Egyptians liked best to eat is shown by the paintings on the walls of the tombs – fruit and vegetables: onions, garlic, leeks, cucumbers, figs, dates, melons, grapes, and in the Late Period also apples, pomegranates and olives. Next to them lie geese, pigeons, cranes. Beef is usually represented by an ox leg. Since Egyptian meat could not be kept, slaughtered animals had to be consumed within a few days. In the workers' village of Deir el-Medinah, meat was only distributed on the most important holidays and then from the animals sacrificed to the gods in the temple. Archaeologists found a real, complete meal, rather than a painted one, in a tomb in Saqqara. From the dried remains, chemists could reconstruct the entire menu, apart from two items. It was served on clay crockery: bread, brewed barley, a cooked fish, a cooked quail (with its head under its wing), pigeon stew, two cooked kidneys, ox ribs and leg, followed by berries, stewed fruit (probably figs), small round cakes sweetened with honey and several types of cheese. Nearby stood a large jug of wine. This sumptuous meal was set out for the underworld for a woman from the 2nd Dynasty a good 500 years ago. The chemists cannot say exactly what the recipes were and the Egyptians themselves did not leave one single cooking or baking recipe. However, we do know

that they baked 35 different sorts of bread and cakes and can conclude that variations in these baked delicacies were one of their small everyday pleasures. How they tasted, no one can tell.

A Sociable Life – And Love

As a rule, the Egyptians ate three times a day. In the morning they partook of a breakfast called "mouthwashing", mostly alone. For lunch and especially for the evening meal, called "rising of the stars", they met with their family or friends. A joyful get-together was one of the pleasures of life, as shown by painted banquets in the tombs. "To please the heart, to rejoice in pleasure, to take part in good things, a lotus blossom on my nose, and myrrh as unguent on my locks" is written next to the festive picture in the tomb of the vizier Rekhmira. He had eaten and drunk a huge amount. "Enjoy the day," sang the blind harpist to those at the feast, "while the woman of your heart is sitting next to you."
Tomb painting was very discreet in the depiction of love and erotica, with only the woman's arm laid around the shoulder or back of the man (never the other way round!) giving a clue. Perhaps the harp playing of young girls was seen as the prelude to "hanky-panky". The Egyptians probably associated erotic pleasure with painted bowers or with hunting scenes in reed thickets, accompanied by women. Explicit representations are missing in the burial chambers. The situation is different in pictures, which were presumably produced for the pleasure of the artist and his friends.
A papyrus stored in a Turin museum, clay fragments with sketches or small clay figures show that at that time fantasies also knew no bounds. However, these representations lay outside the confines of official art with its strict rules of form. On temple walls we see mostly the erect penis of the god Min, under whose protection came all forms of fertility. A broader view was taken of love and sex in literature than in painting; there were many love songs, not only about

Socialising was one of the pleasures of life: Lady May is laying her arm tenderly around the shoulders of her husband Amenhotep, a high official and brother of the host, the vizier Ramose.
Relief in the tomb of Ramose, Thebes No. 55, 18th Dynasty

Presumably artists created such clearly erotic representations for their own pleasure. There were none among grave goods, possibly because it was feared that they could get out of control.
Cairo, Egyptian Museum

The sexual organs were hardly ever shown in official highly-stylised temple art. Only the fertility god Min and the resurrected Osiris appear with an erect penis.
Relief in the White Chapel of Sesostris I, Karnak, 12th Dynasty

A woman squatting on the bed next to her husband, playing the harp – a discreet hint at sexual pleasures.
Tomb of Mereruka, Saqqara, Old Kingdom, 6th Dynasty

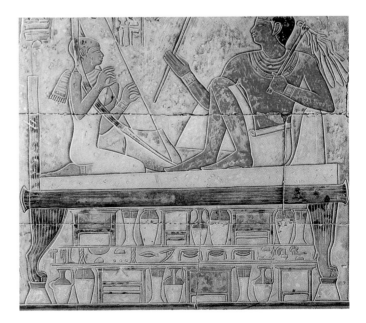

pain and longing, but also happiness and ecstasy. By comparison, descriptions are handed down such as: "You sit in the tavern, surrounded by prostitutes; you want to become tender and enjoy yourself. You tarry with the girls and are bathed in oil, a garland of herbs round your neck and you are drumming on your belly!"

Belly drumming was regarded as a sign of being wildly uninhibited. As in other cultures, erotic pleasure is almost always depicted from the male perspective. In a fairy tale a priest advised the bored King Seneferu thus: "May Your Majesty wend his way to the palace lake. Man your boat with the most beautiful of your palace attendants. Your Majesty's heart will quicken, when you see them rowing up and down, and when you look at the beautiful birds' nests by your lake and the surrounding pastures and beaches, your heart will be glad." The priest also had

Two royal children walking in the garden. They are looking at one another and the girl is giving the boy flowers. We only find such natural representations of tender feelings in the short reign of Akhenaten.
Relief picture of a royal couple, artist's sketch on limestone, Amarna, 18th Dynasty, 25 x 20 cm, Berlin, Egyptian Museum

"twenty women fetched, who have not yet given birth, with flawless bodies and young breasts and plaited hair," gave them "nets made of pearls instead of clothes [...] they rowed up and down, and it did the king's heart good, to see them rowing."

At the painted banquets, there are also naked women "who have not yet given birth" and scantily clad female musicians accompanying young female dancers performing acrobatic exercises. The pleasure the Egyptians took in beautiful bodies cannot be overestimated. Even in official processions, female acrobats and dancers of the goddess of love Hathor took part dressed only in a short apron, rounded at the front.

"I was one of those who loved being drunk, a man of the good days," is written on the coffin of the Osiris priest Wennofer. He enthuses over "dancing girls" and "women dressed in veils with perfect bodies, long curls and taut breasts [...] I followed my love into the garden and wandered at will through the bird ponds [...]," and he wanted to carry on.

As much as the Egyptians hoped to take the pleasures of life with them into the underworld, conversely they were also clearly aware of the threat of the underworld while still in this life. According to Herodotus, although he visited Egypt at the time of its decline, at banquets "after the meal, a man carries in a wooden picture of a corpse lying in a coffin. It

Hunting in the papyrus thicket in female company was probably a metaphor for an erotic relationship.
Wall-painting from the tomb of Nebamun, Thebes No. 90, 18th Dynasty, London, British Museum

is beautifully formed and painted [...] he holds it up to his drinking friends and says: "look at him and drink and be merry! When you are dead, you will be like him!"

Female dancers and acrobats entertaining guests at a banquet. They are showing off their thin, almost naked bodies, "which have not yet given birth". An anonymous artist has drawn on an ostracon a long-haired, slender girl doing a backwards somersault.
From Thebes, 19th Dynasty, limestone, painted, 10.5 cm x 16.8 cm, Turin, Museo Egizio

merut = love

Anubis, the jackal-headed god of the necropolis, bends over the mummy. There are pictures similar to this in many tombs. In reality specialist priests took care of the proper conservation of the corpse and the magic rites connected with it.
Tomb of Nebenmaat, tomb worker from Deir el-Medinah, Thebes No. 219, 20th Dynasty

Survival Techniques – Mummies

sah = mummy

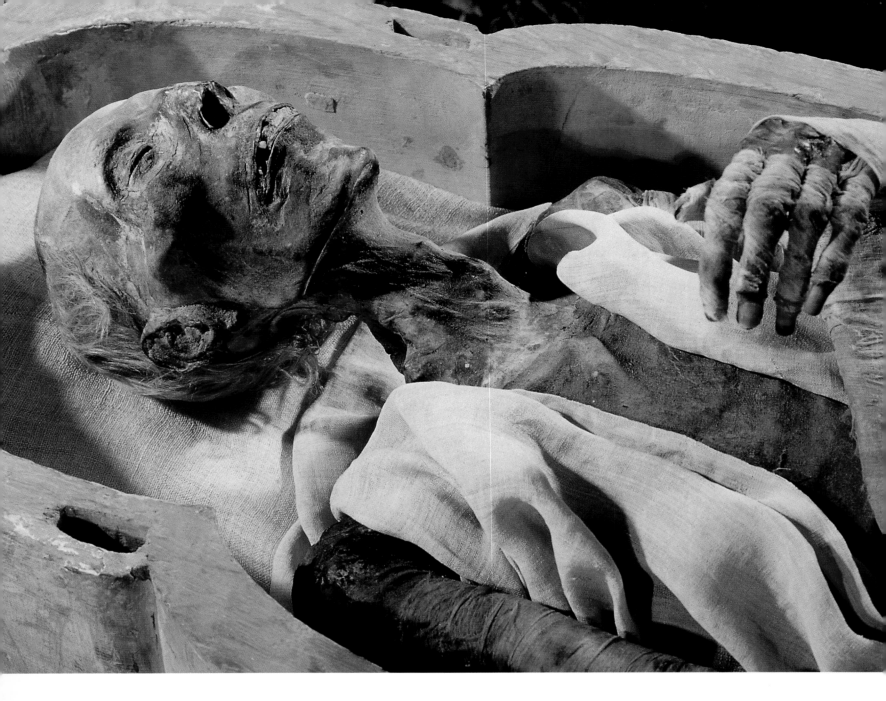

The pharaoh Ramesses II had survived unscathed for almost 3,000 years, thanks to the Egyptian art of embalming and preservation in the desert, but after a few decades in the museum the mummy was at risk of disintegration. French scientists were able to save it.
Cairo, Egyptian Museum

It was every Egyptian's wish to be carried as a mummy to the god of death Osiris on the back of the bull Apis. The hieroglyphs name the donor of the stele as Nesamun, priest of the Theban god Montu.
Funerary stele, Vienna, Kunsthistorisches Museum

The perfect mummy is as light as a blown egg and hard as a statue, according to experts. As "bodies for eternity", they have to survive for "millions of years". Today, the bodily remains of the Egyptians confront us with the transitoriness of man and the age-old wish to elude it. Mummification arose out of the Egyptians' belief in the underworld: it meant that the soul freed in death had a place to which it could return, if the body was preserved. "I will not decay" is written on one coffin, "my body will not be eaten by worms […] it is long lasting, it will not be destroyed in this country throughout eternity." The fact that in the 1970's the most famous mummy of all, that of the pharaoh Ramesses II was in danger of decay, was due solely to the climatic conditions in the Cairo Museum, not to that excellent specialist, who had carried out the treatment in 1212 B.C. At that time, after thousands of years of experimentation, the Egyptian embalming technique was at its peak.

A gold mask protected the head and chest of Tutankhamun's mummy, when those who discovered him opened and photographed the innermost coffin. A floral wreath had been put around the neck of the king, who died young, as decoration.
Photo from 1923

The perfect mummy should be as light as a blown egg and hard as a statue.
Unclothed mummy of a boy, Leiden, Rijksmuseum van Oudheden

The most expensive way of preparing a mummy took up to 70 days. The work was carried out in the embalming halls close to the Nile.

Funerary tub of the Amun priest Djedhoriufankh, from Thebes, Third Interim Period, Cairo, Egyptian Museum

At the Place of Purification

Before this technique was developed, the Egyptians took care of their dead by wrapping them in a mat or animal skin and burying them in the sand. Due to the heat and ventilation provided by the desert wind, many of them dried out before decay could set in. They later wanted to reproduce this natural conservation artificially. The embalming took 70 days and was carried out on the west bank of the Nile away from the residential areas. Next the bodies were put in airy tents close to the river bank, because for washing them water was needed – there are still remnants of aquatic plants clinging to some mummies. Then they were taken to embalming halls, known as the "House of Beauty" or "Place of Purification".

The work was carried out by priests, who performed mystical-religious acts. While doing this, if representations are to be believed, they wore masks which were reproductions of Anubis, the jackal or canine-headed god of the dead. For the tutelary god of the necropolis, the Egyptians had deliberately chosen that animal which prowls around threatening to dig up the dead; by doing this they hoped to placate him. The single preserved specimen of an Anubis mask is made of clay and has eye slits. Perhaps these served as breathing aids. As the embalmers were sometimes careless and left tools (and once a mouse) inside the mummy, we know what instruments they used in their work: bronze hooks, tweezers, spoons, needles and forked awls for opening, emptying and closing up the body again, together with a pot with a spout for pouring the warm consecrated oil.

Did the funerary priests use masks such as this to aid breathing, thus turning themselves into the jackal-headed god of death? Possibly this one remaining specimen, weighing 8 kg, was used only as a model for lighter masks made from cartonnage.
Clay Anubis mask, provenance unknown, Late Period, height 40 cm, Hildesheim, Pelizaeus-Museum

wabet = place of purification

Two lions create a small embalming table, used for preparing the internal organs. Blood and bodily fluids could flow into the bowl held by the lion's tails.
From Saqqara, Old Kingdom, calcite, length 89 cm, height 38 cm, Cairo, Egyptian Museum

An Eye-Witness Account

The Egyptians did not keep written records of embalming techniques, as they did not usually document technical processes such as pyramid and tomb building (or even keep cooking recipes). We have to rely on the descriptions of a foreigner, Herodotus, the Greek with a thirst for knowledge. According to Herodotus, after the general wailing over the deceased had begun, the corpse was taken to professional embalmers. They "showed a choice of wooden bodies painted in various ways", some reasonably priced and others more expensive. Once one had been chosen and the price agreed, the relatives returned home and the embalmers got down to work.

"The most refined method is as follows: first of all they draw out the brain through the nostrils with an iron hook [...] then they make an incision in the flank with a sharp Ethiopian stone through which they extract all the internal organs. They then clean out the body cavity, rinsing it with palm wine and pounded spices. Then they fill the stomach with pure pounded myrrh [...] and stitch it up again."

Afterwards the corpse was covered with natron for 70 days. "After the 70 days are up, they wash the corpse, and wrap it from head to toe in bandages of the finest linen anointed with gum, which the Egyptians use in place of glue. Finally they hand over the body to the relatives who place it in a wooden coffin in the shape of a man. It is then shut up in the family burial chamber [...]."

Herodotus also describes a simpler method of embalming. The bodies were not cut open, but filled with cedarwood oil injected through the anus, which decomposed the internal organs. Scientific investigations have largely confirmed what Herodotus says. Their findings are as follows: on the fourth

For a long time the embalming process was a closely guarded secret. This coffin lid from the Late Period shows it in several scenes, which are read from bottom to top. On the underside of the coffin is the elegant shape of Imentet, the tutelary goddess of tombs. *Lid and underside of the coffin of Djedbastetiuefankh, Ptolemaic Period, sycamore with stucco-covered canvas outer garment, Hildesheim, Pelizaeus-Museum*

keres = coffin

Anubis also kept watch in Tutankhamun's tomb. He lay in an ante-room on a shrine, decorated with gold and precious stones. *Wooden statue from the tomb of Tutankhamun, Valley of the Kings, Thebes, 18th Dynasty, height 118 cm, Cairo, Egyptian Museum*

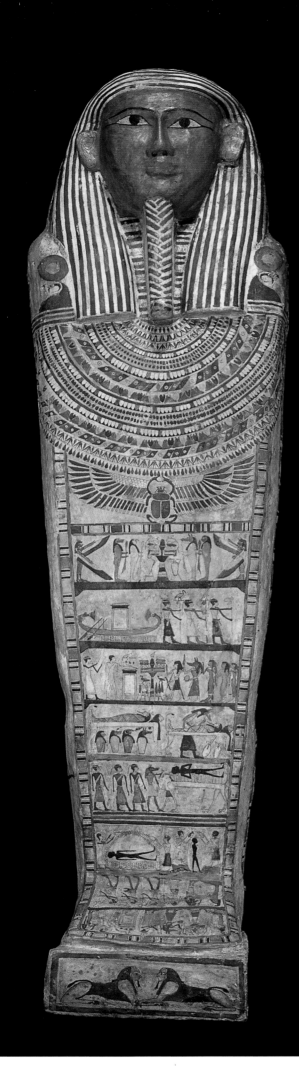

day after death, the embalmers began work; the chemical drying-out took 52 days and 16 days were set aside for the wrapping, then the mummy was laid in the coffin and buried after three days. Natron solution, as reported by Herodotus, was only used in early times, however. From the Middle Kingdom they used the more effective natron powder. This chemical (Na_2Co_3 + $NaHCo_3$) was widely available in Egypt in the Wadi Natrun, a desert valley, that also gave natron its name. Several times the body weight of the corpse in natron was packed around the corpse; it could be used several times, but with diminishing effectiveness. Sacks of natron powder have been found in the burial chambers and can also occasionally be seen in pictures under the embalming table.

The exact composition of the substance that Herodotus called "gum", the consecrated oil, with which the bandages were impregnated, remains unclear, because the various ingredients have undergone chemical reactions with each other over the course of thousands of years. They are plant oils, mixed with fragrant plant resins (conifer resin, imported from the Lebanon, incense and myrrh), which were anti-bacterial and effective in killing off fungi. They hardened the emptied, dehydrated, now light body, which occasionally stuck to the coffin bottom. This was

Representation on the coffin of Djedbastetiuefankh. The first scene shows a purification priest pouring different liquids over the naked body as preparation for embalming.

ut = embalmer

◯ = boil ("sign of loathing")

the case with Tutankhamun. When the consecrated oil was chiselled away from under his body, the mummy broke up into many pieces.

The artistically wrapped bandages were examined by textile research scientists. They measured up to 375 square metres of linen on one mummy, noticed a preference for the colours red or pink, and found out that new linen was by no means always used. They presume that in most Egyptian houses there was a drawer with discarded, carefully darned clothes, from which mummy bandages were made when needed. "He who owned so much fine linen," says one old death lament, "[...] is now sleeping in yesterday's cast-offs."

Second scene: The naked body is lying on the embalming table which is decorated with lion's feet. A priest wearing an Anubis mask is holding bandages in his hands to begin the wrapping, with his assistants behind him.

Third scene: the Canopic jars containing the internal organs stand under the wrapped mummy. As always the priest, or Anubis himself, is bent over the final stages of the work in a stereotyped pose.

Magical Reinforcement

The mummies from the Old and Middle Kingdoms have hardly any body tissue left and, on being unwrapped, crumble more or less into dust. For the technique of perfect embalming, such as we know from the mummies of the New Kingdom, Ramesses II is the most famous example. Poor people were of course still wrapped in an ox skin and buried in the desert. At first the nobility were buried in a box-shaped coffin, which was laid in a stone sarcophagus. In the Middle Kingdom the practice of shaping the wooden coffins into a human form began, and these then became increasingly popular. Over the face of the mummies themselves was laid a mask of stuccoed linen, which however bore no similarity to how the deceased had actually looked, something which was not striven for until Roman times. The well-protected mummy was laid at an angle on its side, so that it could look to the east, where the living resided. The eyes, which were painted on one side of the outer coffin, could only open if someone like the artist Neferhotep in Deir el-Medinah spoke the correct texts while the painting was being carried out.

For, however much trouble the Egyptians took over the process of conserving the body, over clean disembowelling, over the chemicals, natron, resins, oil, and over a refined wrapping technique for preserving the body's shape, this material aspect of mummification was only a part of the procedure. It was completely ineffective without support from the secret art of the magician.

During the 70 days of embalming – this period was for religious rather than technical reasons – the high priests ensured that each time the correct spells were read out and the appropriate rituals took place. A priest recited the incantations, evoked the names of the gods and placed

A quadruple *wadjet*-eye.
Late Period, Hildesheim, Pelizaeus-Museum

Amulets, to which the Egyptians attributed magic powers, were wrapped up with the mummies. The *wadjet*-eye (*wadjet* =sound, undamaged) was supposed to divert disaster from the dead.
Late Period, Hildesheim, Pelizaeus-Museum

The heart was considered to be the centre of the personality, the seat of the will and understanding, and was weighed by the gods in the underworld. The red heart amulet was supposed to help in this test.
Hildesheim, Pelizaeus-Museum

The "knot of Isis" amulet takes the form of the hieroglyph for life (*ankh*), one of the most important symbols, which we see the gods handing over to people in many representations.

In the Middle Kingdom coffins were made in the shape of humans, and covered with a stylised portrait of the deceased. The painted wooden coffin of Madja comes from

the tomb workers' village, Deir el-Medinah.
New Kingdom, length 184 cm, Paris, Musée du Louvre

the dead under their personal protection. "You will be improved by gold [...]," he said to the dead, "you are walking on your feet to the House of Eternity." For "gold is the meat of the gods" and confers longevity.

The lengthy procedure of wrapping was also accompanied by holy spells. At the same time, amulets were placed amongst the bandages to protect the dead – up to 87 for a single corpse. A particularly important amulet, the eye of Horus, closed the incision through which the embalmer had removed the internal organs of the corpse, as a sign that it was intact. The belly had been filled with fragrant plants or wood shavings beforehand, mixed with pepper corns or juniper berries and onions. The Egyptians believed that onions – just like garlic – would keep away evil forces.

Since gold is the "flesh of the gods", the incision through which the embalmer removed the internal organs from the body was closed up with a gold disc. It was also decorated with the wadjet-eye, the sign of intactness.
Gold disc from the tomb of the pharaoh Psusennes I, from Tanis (Nile Delta), 21st Dynasty, width 16.6 cm, Cairo, Egyptian Museum

heka = magic

The liver, lungs, spleen, stomach and intestines were also entrusted to the protection of the gods. They went in the tomb and were kept safe in four containers, the Canopic jars, decorated with the heads of people, baboons, falcons and jackals.
Canopic jars, Late Period, height ca. 30 cm, Hildesheim, Pelizaeus-Museum

The goddess of the sky, Nut, spreads out her arms protectively to receive the deceased. He is sheltered by her, is absorbed into her body, and emerges reborn.
Floor of a sarcophagus from Saqqara, Ptolemaic Period, Cairo, Egyptian Museum

djed = eternity

Gods – Protectors of the Dead

Near the coffins in the graves there are always other containers to be found, mostly wooden boxes, in which four vessels were kept, from the simple clay pot to the artistically shaped alabaster vase. The Egyptians called them Canopic jars after the town of Canopus, which lies to the east of Alexandria. They were used to hold the internal organs taken from the body and, because the body was incomplete without them, these were always placed together.

The oldest Canopic box, an alabaster block containing wrapped organ remains, dates from the 4th Dynasty of the Old Kingdom. It belonged to Hetepheres, the mother of the famous pyramid builder Cheops. What was at first customary only among kings and queens was soon being imitated by the high officials, and in the New Kingdom by all well-off Egyptians. The liver, stomach, lungs and intestines were wrapped up individually in linen, the packages were put into Canopic vessels, resinous consecrated oil was poured over them, and then they were closed and conserved for "eternity". The brain, on the other hand, was thrown away, clearly being considered unimportant. The heart was where the Egyptians located the spirit, understanding and senses. Being of such crucial importance, the heart was always put back into the mummified body immediately after the preserving treatment. The dead needed it as an adviser in the courts of the underworld. The precious internal organs were entrusted to divine protection, to the four sons of Horus, whose heads usually adorn the stoppers of the Canopic vessels. The human-headed Amset (which means "dill", a herb which is still popular for its preserving properties) watches over the stomach; Hapi, with the head of a baboon, protects the intestines; Duamutef looks like a dog and is responsible for the lungs and Qebehsenuf, with the head of a falcon, guards the liver. In the New Kingdom, another four goddesses of protection are depicted at the corners of the Canopic boxes. They also watch – with outstretched wings – over the contents. The same goddesses also kneel at the corners of the large sarcophagi and are again portrayed on the human-shaped coffins. Nut, the goddess of the sky, is often stretched out on the inside of the coffin lid, her starry body covering and protecting the dead. These are the gods who protect mankind, their bodies and their internal organs from transitoriness, and without them the best embalming techniques remain ineffective.

A Guide through
the Underworld

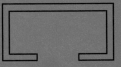

duat = underworld

An Egyptian burial was a real party – the highlight of existence and an event for which everybody made preparations and saved throughout their whole life. They had their tombs built and decorated in good time, ordered the coffin and bought the best of all the various things from life that they wanted to take with them into the underworld. A whole branch of industry dealt with the manufacture of these tomb furnishings and a considerable part of the gross national product disappeared underground in this way. However, the investment seemed to make sense, as this was the only way to ensure an after-life. The after-life was dependent on the body carrying on and satisfying its everyday needs such as eating and drinking, and having somewhere to live.

For foreign "wretched" peoples, who were not aware of these precautionary measures, a "definitive" death was certain. "Return to Egypt!" writes the pharaoh to his subject Sinuhe, who lived in exile abroad. "You shall not die in a foreign land! / The Asians shall not bury you! / […] Think of your body and return!" His advice was followed. Sinuhe was mummified after his death in accordance with all the rules of the art of embalming and interred with a splendid funeral in the "beautiful west".

In the west of Egyptian towns, where the sun sets and the desert begins, the great tomb sites, the necropolises, lie, separated from but within sight of the living. Lying at the foot of the pyramids at Memphis are Saqqara, Giza, Abu Sir and other burial sites. At Thebes the necropolis lies on the west bank of the Nile, under a mountain peak shaped like a pyramid. There the goddess of the west, Imentet, "she who loves the silence", and the jackal-headed god Anubis keep watch.

The funeral procession would make its way to the necropolis. The embalming procedure lasted 70 days, and the mummy then lay in the open, richly decorated coffin, as the pharaoh so enticingly described it to the exiled Sinuhe: "the sky is above you, while you lie on a bier. Oxen pull you

A marvellous funeral procession: oxen pull the sledge through the desert, the mummy lies in an open coffin on a bier, protected by two goddesses.
Papyrus from the Book of the Dead of Maiherperi, 18th Dynasty, Cairo, Egyptian Museum

A group of female mourners, wailing, with loose hair and naked breasts, were part of every "proper funeral" – although they were not cheap, as a bill verifies.
Tomb of Ramose, Thebes No. 55, 18th Dynasty

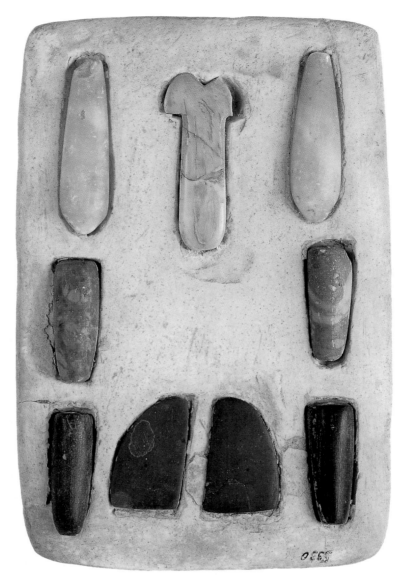

These instruments from the Old Kingdom, with which the priests carried out the "Opening of the Mouth" ceremony, were adapted from the tools of the coffin makers and embalmers. They can also be seen on the table in front of Tutankhamun.
Opening-of-the-mouth set, 17.5 cm x 11.5 cm, University of Leipzig, Egyptian Museum

along, musicians lead the way […]." Slowly the coffin was pulled on a sledge by a team of oxen through the desert sand, followed by family and friends, by priests waving incense and by wailing mourners with loose hair and bare breasts. Slaves carried the grave goods, furniture, clothes boxes, jewellery and cosmetic articles. They also brought meat, poultry and vegetables for the death sacrifice. That the amount paid for sweet things, bread, wreaths of flowers and fragrant cones was small, is verified by the bill for a funeral in the 2nd century B.C. The mourners on the other hand were expensive, but the bandages and cloths, preserving oils and resins needed for the embalming cost far more.

The mummy was taken out of the coffin in front of the tomb and stood up, held by an embalming priest wearing an Anubis mask. A lay priest, usually the oldest son, burned incense, while the lector priest read out magic spells from a papyrus scroll. The magic "Opening of the Mouth" ritual was celebrated with the tools of the coffin maker and embalmer, an adze, a knife and a special device shaped like a fish tail. The priests opened the mummy's mouth, eyes, ears and nose, so that the dead person regained the power of their senses and could accept food sacrifices. They were

"born again" in a mysterious, costly ceremony, that could last several days in the case of high-ranking people and was re-enacted in the statues and pictures, which went into the tomb with them.

Now the family could take their leave of the dead person, and the mummy was replaced in the coffin, equipped for the underworld. Death sacrifices were offered, for example ritually slaughtered and barbecued oxen, and then consumed by the family during the death feast at the tomb. In Thebes, this was repeated every year in the New Kingdom at the "beautiful banquet of the desert valley", a sort of Egyptian "All Saints", where sacrifices were made and joyful celebrations took place on and in the tombs.

Bread and Cool Water

The dead stayed behind as master of their beautiful "House of Eternity". Over the course of three thousand years the architecture of the tombs changed, from pyramids and mastaba to tombs cut out of rock, but two main elements remained the same: the sarcophagus and the concealed, subterranean chamber in which it was hidden. In front of this there was a room, a place of worship, accessible from outside, with a stone tablet, a stele on which the name and possibly a picture of the dead person was recorded, and the offering table. A "false door", a stone imitation of a real door, made the ideal link between the two places, between this world and the underworld. It was only accessible to the deceased; they alone could stride through it to receive the sacrificial offering. Bread, vegetables, fruit, poultry and, on feast days, meat were brought as offerings. Particularly welcome was incense for the nose and beer or cool water, because they lived on the edge of the desert. Their children had to supply them regularly with these things. Often the deceased had also established a foundation "for eternity" while they were still alive. In this case, mortuary priests were responsible for its provision and they and the temple lived well from it, since the offerings ended up on their table.

But hard times showed the Egyptians, particularly in the chaotic "Intermediate Periods", that even "eternal" foundations fade away, so to provide for these times of want the sacrificial offerings were also painted on the wall or written down. People trusted in the magic of pictures and writing. Even the spoken word could be powerful, a living person just naming the offerings being sufficient to provide for the needs of the deceased. This explains the plea which can be read on so many memorial stones, "Oh you, who live on earth and pass by this stele [...] if you love life and hate death, say: may he receive a thousand loaves of bread and a thousand jugs of beer!"

The party is over, the guests have departed and the mourning woman sits alone in front of the tomb entrance, tearing at her hair. This small scene was discovered on a tomb stele, which shows the donor in front of an offering table and the god Re-Horakhte.
Wooden stele of Djedamuniuankh from Deir el-Bahari, 22nd Dynasty, height 27.6 cm, Cairo, Egyptian Museum

ka = soul, spirit, life-force

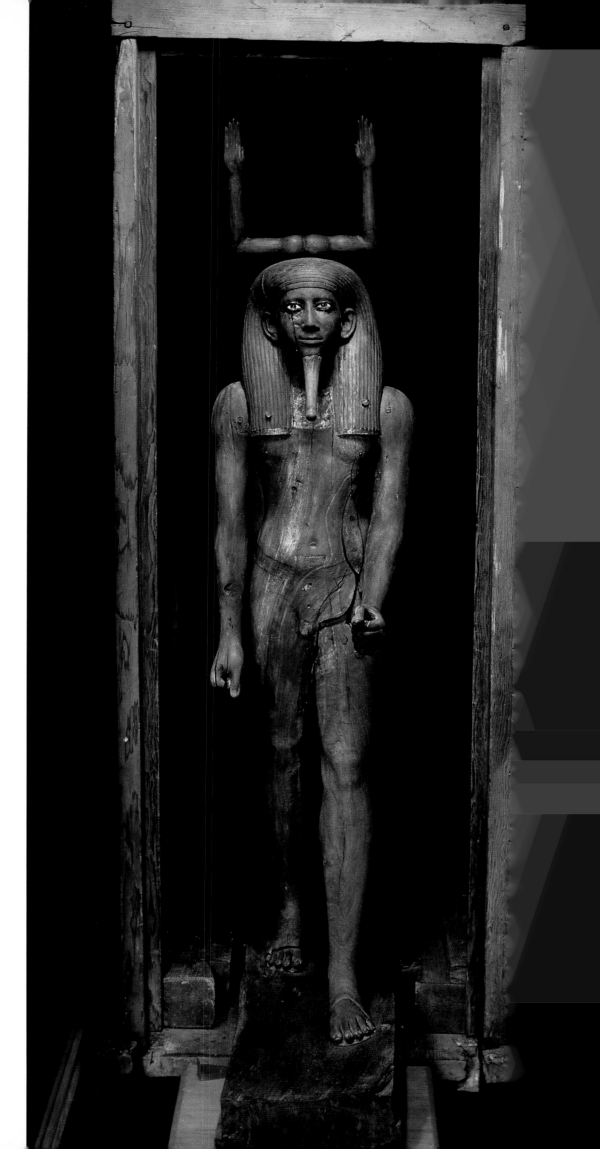

Entrance of the king Auyibre Hor.
The raised hands fixed onto his
head, the hieroglyph of Ka, show
the statue to be the ka of the dead
man, his energy and life-force.
If his mummy should be destroyed,
the king would be able to take up
residence in this statue. Food was
brought as a sacrificial offering.
Wooden statue from Dahshur,
Middle Kingdom, 13th Dynasty,
height 170 cm, Cairo, Egyptian
Museum

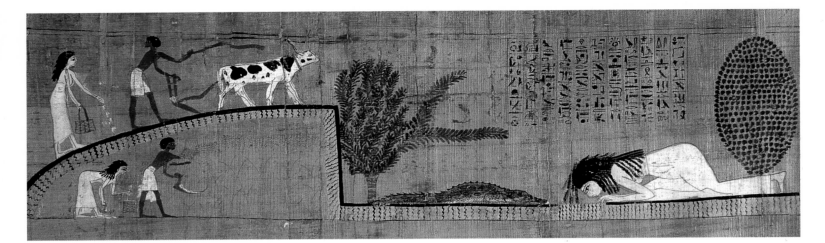

Fresh water was a requirement for the dead in the desert. In this vignette the "singer of Amun" Hereubechet is drinking from a river, before she sows and harvests in the Field of Reeds.
From a Book of the Dead from Deir el-Bahari, 21st Dynasty, Cairo, Egyptian Museum

The deceased could come through the false door of his burial chamber in different guises in order to feast on the sacrificial offerings, since the Egyptians were not satisfied with the simple duality of body and soul. They considered the identity of a person to be made up of many components: the body, which was preserved from decay by mummification – if all went well – and was linked to the other parts of the being. If it disintegrated or was burnt he would also be destroyed – if no statue had been placed in the tomb as a replacement for such an emergency. This did not have to resemble the deceased physically, but had to bear his name, as that was an important part of the person, without which there was no individuality, no chance of survival.

Even the shadow belongs to a person, and that which we simply call the soul was differentiated by the Egyptians into Ka, Ba and Akh. The Ka is the energy and life force, which are the vital roots. The sacrificial offerings were meant for the Ka, since it needs food. It is created at birth by the creator-god Khnum on the potter's wheel and never leaves. It is represented by two raised arms.

The Ba corresponds most closely to our idea of "soul"; it can detach itself from the body but must return to it. It appears as a bird with a human head, sitting in the branches of the sycamore tree near the tomb or fluttering around it: "You swoop up and down [...] / you glide where your heart desires, / you come out of your tomb every morning, / you return every evening."

This mobility, the deceased coming out of their tombs, also holds dangers: a third aspect of the soul is called Akh and can haunt the living as a kind of spirit. A widower from the New Kingdom implores in a letter "to the excellent spirit Anchiri", his dead wife, to please leave him in peace, otherwise he will "lodge a complaint with the gods of the west". For there are judges in the underworld as well and before a deceased person can be accepted there, he must appear before them – complete with all the different parts of his being.

The shadow was also a part of the person. It appears here as a dark silhouette and is bound to the dead person in the tomb like the Ka, but unlike the Ba – a further aspect of their individuality – which is represented as a fluttering bird with a human head.
Tomb of Irinufer, Thebes No. 290, Ramesside Period

Led by Anubis, the craftsman Sennedjem steps into the kingdom of the dead, where tests and dangers are awaiting him.
Tomb of Sennedjem, Thebes No. 1, 19th Dynasty

Books of the Dead were used as guides in the underworld.
They supplied the magic spells with which the deceased could justify themselves. At the Court of the Dead the heart of the deceased was weighed against a feather, the symbol of divine order.
If it proved to be too heavy, it was devoured by the "Swallowing Monster".
Papyrus Any, 18th Dynasty, London, British Museum

The Judgement of the Dead

The panel of judges sits in the "hall of complete justness", where this world and the underworld coincide. Here there is a large scales, on which the heart of the deceased is weighed under the supervision of the jackal-headed Anubis and Thoth, the god of writing. The Egyptians regarded the heart as the centre of the personality, as the seat of understanding, will and conscience. On the other side of the scales lies a feather, symbol of the goddess of justice Maat, and of the divine order. The deceased has only passed the test when the heart is as light as the feather.

The earthly behaviour of a person is therefore measured here against the ideal of heavenly justice. Only a very small number of people would have been a match for such a test. Everyone was afraid of it, as next to the scales was the

"Great Swallower", a monster made up of a crocodile, big cat and hippopotamus, ready to devour those whose hearts proved to be too heavy. That would be the worst of all imaginable punishments, total annihilation, the final second death with no hope of rebirth. But even here the Egyptians made provision during their lifetime.

Papyrus scrolls lay between the legs of many mummies, wrapped into the linen bandages. They contained spells and pictures, a kind of guide through the kingdom of the dead. In earlier times, in the Old Kingdom, they were chiselled onto the walls of the secret burial chambers in the pyramids for the exclusive use of the kings. These "Pyramid texts" are among the oldest known theological texts. A certain "democratisation process", at least as far as the underworld was concerned, later also permitted well-off civil servants to equip themselves for the kingdom of the dead with instruc-

tions, the useful spells being written on their coffins and, in the New Kingdom, on papyrus scrolls. These "Books of the Dead" could be bought complete, leaving only the name of the owner to be inserted. They cost approximately the same as one or two cows, one slave or half-a-year's income for a worker, and thus remained inaccessible to the lower classes.

The guide to the underworld – written by Thoth himself, the god of wisdom – did not only name the dangers of the underworld, but at the same time had a set of incantations compiled in a kind of magic book to tone them down. There were about 200 magic formulae, which, spoken at the right moment, could help the owner. When appearing before the court of the dead and the weighing ceremony for instance, the 125th spell could be recited; it began "I have not acted evilly towards anyone," continued "I have not

mistreated any animals" and "I have not stopped the flow of water at its seasons." This did not have to correspond with the truth, and was frankly often used to prevent the truth coming to light. The text served as an entreaty, through which, entranced by the spells and the magic pictures on the papyrus, the scales would stay in balance and the judges pronounce the deceased in accord with the divine order: "He is justified. The Swallowing Monster shall have no power over him!"

In the Kingdom of Osiris

As head of the Court of the Dead and ruler over the underground kingdom sits Osiris, the "Lord of Eternity". He was originally a fertility god: his face is green, like the primeval mud, out of which all life comes, and like the Nile, whose inundation makes the land fertile, year in, year out. He wears the insignia of power: crown, crook, flail and sceptre, but his body is stiff, immobile, a wrapped-up, artistically painted mummy. This means that although he is a mighty god, Osiris remains subject to human fate. Like his subjects

he must also die and the great hope of mankind is based on this common destiny. The good king Osiris, according to Egyptian legend, was of divine origin and ruled the land wisely. However, he had a hostile brother, Seth, who killed him, dismembered the body and threw it in the Nile. Isis, the sister-wife of Osiris, looked for him. "Sorrowfully she passed through the land and did not take rest until she had found him." Anubis joined all 14 parts of the body together and wrapped them in bandages, thus making the first mummy. Isis changed herself into a female hawk and "produced air with her wings". Then the dead god began to come back to

Osiris is the highest judge in the Court of the Dead. As ruler of the underworld he wears the insignia of power: crown, flail and crook, but he has the immobile body of a mummy.
Tomb of Sennedjem, Thebes No. 1, 19th Dynasty

The resurrected Osiris, murdered by his brother and brought back to life by his wife Isis, embodies the hope of rebirth.
Osiris statue from Saqqara, Late Period, height 89.5 cm, Cairo, Egyptian Museum

usir = Osiris

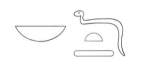

neb djed = Lord of eternity

life, impregnating Isis with a son, Horus, his future heir to the throne. And though Osiris was not allowed to lead his life on earth, he became effective again in the underworld. He became king of the kingdom of the dead. "Now sadness is at an end, laughter has returned."

The Osiris and Isis cult became popular in the Late Period throughout the entire Mediterranean area and even influenced Christianity with its teachings of death and resurrection. Its centre was in Abydos, the most holy ground in Egypt, where the head of Osiris was buried and the Osiris legend was staged as a mystery play to honour the gods.

Small figurines were put into the tomb with the deceased as their representatives. If they were called to work in the underworld, they were to answer for them, "Here I am – Ushabti". They are still called ushabtis today.
Faïence ushabti of Ptahmose from Abydos, New Kingdom, height 20 cm, Cairo, Egyptian Museum

The Egyptian's idea of paradise – the rural idyllic Field of Reeds. Like Sennedjem and his wife, anyone can, after passing certain tests, reserve their field under the protection of the gods.
Tomb of Sennedjem, Thebes No. 1, 19th Dynasty

The corn-Osiris, a clay brick with an image of the god of death sunk into it was filled with earth and grain at funerals. The moistened seeds sprouted – as a symbol of rebirth.
Late Period, height 6 cm, length 21.5 cm, width 10.5 cm, Hildesheim, Pelizaeus-Museum

The Egyptians believed that everything was repeated through the divine order, and therefore everyone should be able to identify with the destiny of the god Osiris, magically fusing with him. Every mortal being hoped to be regenerated and wake up to a different new existence in the underworld. The Book of the Dead guided them safely through the underworld, warning them of the abysses, demons and terrors which lay in wait for them, reflecting exactly the age-old fears of the human soul. A hymn gives a gloomy description of Osiris, telling of "those whose land lies in darkness, whose fields are sand, whose graves serve silence, whose call no one hears, who lie there, unable to rise, whose mummies are swathed in bandages, whose limbs are immobile." The kingdom of the dead is portrayed as a dark and damp place, where the purification and regeneration of the sleepers takes place in the primeval waters; like the corn buried in the earth

they wake up to new life. But then the prayers and entreaty formulae of the Book of the Dead also open the way for the deceased to reach the idyllic "Field of Reeds". There they can till their fields and drink their jug of beer in the evenings or climb into the sun barque to accompany the gods on their journey and with them "go out into the day".

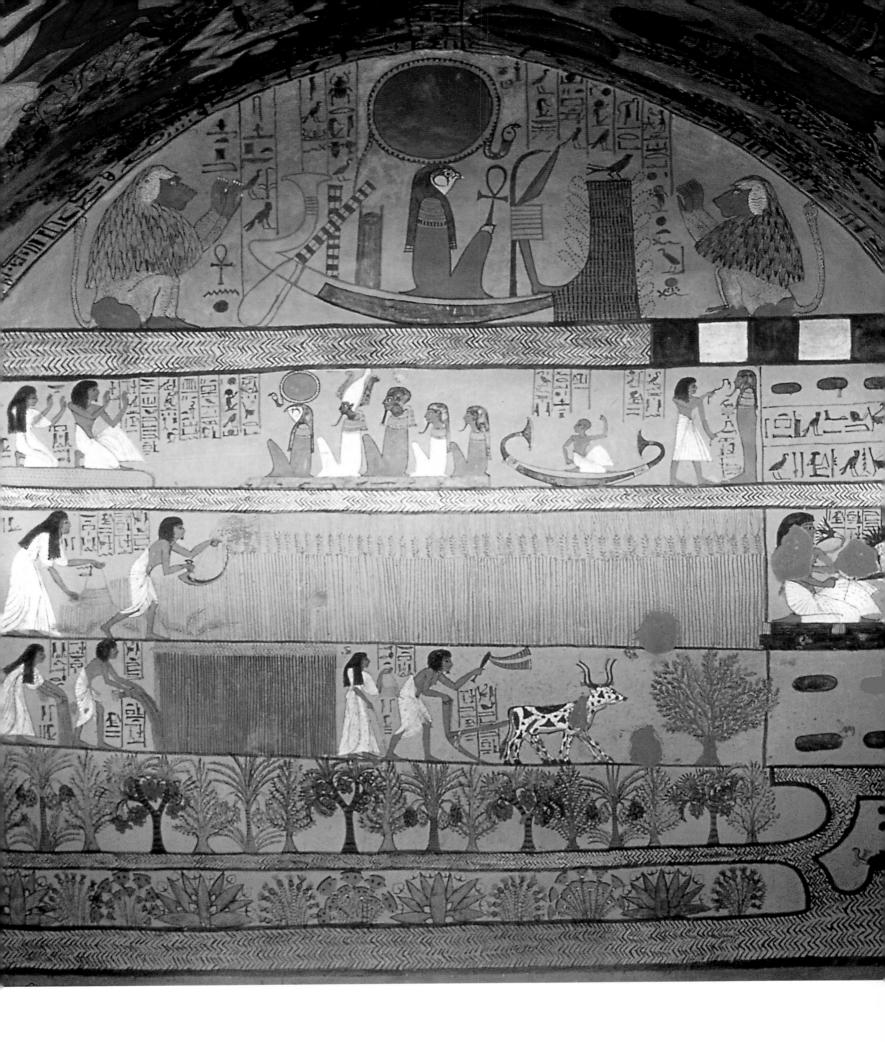

Isis, the "great in magic", was
a powerful tutelary and mother
goddess. This is shown by her
attributes – on her head she wears
the throne, she is kneeling down on
the hieroglyph for gold and is laying
her hand on the ring of eternity.
This relief is part of the decoration
for the stone sarcophagus of Queen
Hatshepsut and the goddess has
taken on her facial features.
From the tomb of Hatshepsut,
Valley of the Kings, Thebes,
New Kingdom, 18th Dynasty

Gods, Goddesses and Magic

netscheru = gods

Two cheering baboons greet the rising sun in the morning, with the falcon-headed god Re-Horakhte in his boat.
Detail from the depiction p. 171, wall-painting from the tomb of Sennedjem, Thebes No. 1, 19th Dynasty

The nocturnal sun barque is pulled through the underworld by the planets. On the boat are two lines of baboons guarding the night sun, with the ram-headed Re.
Relief from the temple of Osiris from Abydos, Merenptah Period, 19th Dynasty

A barque made of pure gold, 770 cubits long, crosses the sky over the Nile every day. It has stars for oars and the gods form its crew. It is the solar barque, under the command of Re, the sun-god, who ensures that life on earth continues by appearing daily with light and heat. As "first among the gods", he rules over mankind, his "flock", and for three thousand years Egypt has paid homage to him as principal and national god. "You are the lord of the sky and the lord of the earth / […] who created the countries and brought forth the peoples / […] heaven and earth greet your countenance!"

At night, Re travels through the kingdom of the dead. Here, planets row the divine barque over the primeval waters Nun, which flow through the underworld. When the barque approaches it becomes light, the dead awake and cheer him, for the sun heralds regeneration and rebirth for them even more strongly than the fertility-god Osiris. The "tired" Osiris represents yesterday, but Re is the morrow. All hope to climb into his barque and to ascend with him out of the underworld participating in the journey across the sky. But before that the divine crew must overcome a series of dangers on the journey through the underworld, for Re's enemy Apophis, a giant dragon-like snake, will try time and time again to capsize their boat, in order to annihilate the gods. This is described in the "Books of the Underworld" in pictures and writing. It is all in vain however, the magic of the gods gathered in the boat proves to be more powerful and Re appears victorious every morning on the eastern horizon, greeted with cheers by baboons.

During the nightly struggle against Apophis, his crew of gods stands by Re, with the ibis-headed god of wisdom and the world, Thoth, acting as his herald. Horus, the falcon-god accompanies him and the aggressive god of chaos Seth and Re's daughter Maat are there, as well as Isis, "who is full of cunning" and Heka, the god of magic, without whose help Apophis could not be overpowered. The exact number in the retinue is not known and the individual gods did not always allow themselves to be identified, as Egyptians believed a god kept the secret of his true shape to himself. It was permissible to make an image of a god, however, providing him with visual attributes. So, just as the Egyptians invented hieroglyphs for objects, names and sounds, they also invented symbols for the different functions of the invisible gods – symbols, not likenesses of the unfathomable deities. They borrowed many of them from the animal kingdom, forming hybrids from man and beast.

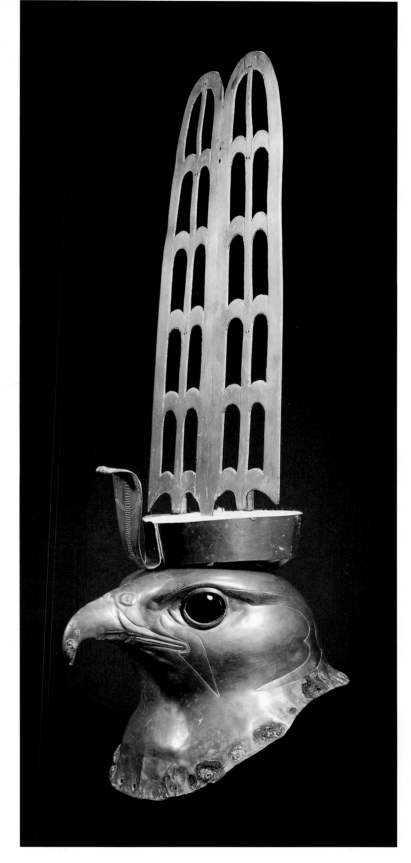

The falcon's head of embossed gold is wearing the uraeus and plumed crown. It was part of a bronze figure of the Horus falcon, tutelary god of Hieraconpolis, the first capital of Upper Egypt.

Falcon head from Hieraconpolis, Old Kingdom, 6th Dynasty, embossed gold and obsidian, height 37.5 cm, Cairo, Egyptian Museum

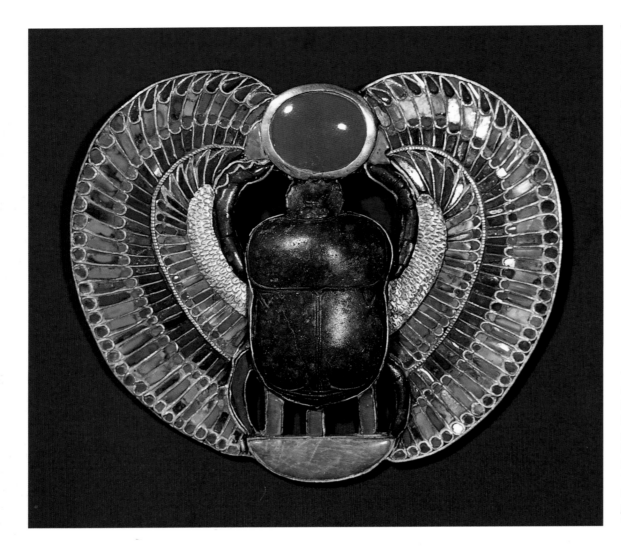

The falcon-headed god of the rising sun, Re-Horakhte, on his throne. He is holding the symbol of life, the *ankh*, and a sceptre in his hand; a snake is protecting the sun-disc on his head. Behind him sits his daughter Hathor, decorated with the hieroglyph for the west, the necropolis. The thrones carry the symbol for the "unity of the two lands".
Painting in the tomb of Queen Nefertari, Valley of the Queens, Thebes, 19th Dynasty

The winged scarab was the symbol of rebirth, because like the dung beetle rolling its eggs before it, it pushes the sun over the horizon every morning. Tutankhamun wore it as an amulet on his chest.
Pendant from the tomb of Tutankhamun, Thebes, Valley of the Kings, 18th Dynasty, gold and precious stones, height 9 cm, width 10.5 cm, Cairo, Egyptian Museum

The Sun:
Beetle, Falcon or Cat?

Re himself is usually represented in human form, although his body is made of gold and on his head he is wearing the "lord of the flames", the sun disc with the fire-spewing uraeus, which protects him from his enemies. His insignia include a head-dress, various royal crowns and sceptres, for he is regarded as the mythical forefather of the pharaohs. But Re is particularly "numerous in names and forms", as the greater the power and responsibilities of a god, the more incarnations he had at his disposal. He appears in human form only at midday and in the evenings; in the morning he can appear as a scarab, that beetle which is continually rolling a ball of dung from which they believed he generated himself. Or he rises in the east as Re-Horakhte, red and with a falcon's head. In the underworld, however, he wears the head of a ram or cuts up his enemy the snake with a knife, in the guise of a large cat.

In the course of his three-thousand-year reign in Egypt, the sun-god has taken on even more forms, either to preserve his power or to extend it. This is first mentioned during the time of the pharaoh Djoser, who built the Step Pyramid. The kings at that time made him the national god and erected sun shrines to him: squares open to the sky, in the centre an altar with a stone, later an obelisk – in the form of a stone sunbeam. The oldest of these sun shrines is in Heliopolis, north-east of Cairo, but it is now almost completely destroyed. There was already a local god called Atum; Re did not drive him away, but joined forces with him. That fits in with the inclination – which we find difficult to comprehend – of the traditionally hidebound Egyptians to be happy to compromise: they did not know "either or", but rather "both and". From these temporary but always advantageous unions came the gods' names, put together in the manner of chemical formulae. So Re became Re-Atum, and hence the creator-god and father of a powerful divine family, the "ennead" of Heliopolis. According to an ancient myth, "ennead" emerged during the creation of the world: at that time a mound of mud was formed from the dark, chaotic primeval waters of Nun and out of it arose Atum, the "all with the mysterious name", in the form of a snake or scarab. He masturbated and begot the first pair of gods from his seed, Tefnut, the goddess of moisture, and Shu, the god of the air and sunlight, who for their part were the parents of Geb, god of the earth, and Nut, the sky-goddess. In a spectacular act, often depicted in Egyptian art, the separation of sky and earth then took

place: the air-god decorated with feathers lifted the star-covered female body of Nut with both arms over the reclining male Geb, and the cosmic order was created. Osiris, Isis, Seth and Nephthys completed this divine family known as the "ennead". Through his "fusion" with Atum, Re had taken the place of the national god, to which he was entitled, in this highly-revered "ennead". This process was repeated when the kingdom was re-unified after the break-up of the Old Kingdom in the 11th Dynasty. People longed for renewal; a new capital, Thebes, was built and there the priesthood launched a king of the gods called Amun. In this way, continuity was preserved; just as Atum had once been fused with Re in Heliopolis, now the young Amun was united with the old national god Re to become Amun-Re. Temples were built to him in Karnak and from then onwards he played a leading role in Ancient Egyptian history. That did not prevent Re remaining active in his original form as sun-god at the same time. As Re from Heliopolis, together with Amun of Thebes and Ptah of Memphis, he formed a trinity, the official Egyptian national triad. An attempt to disturb this balance of the gods in favour of Re was doomed to failure. It was undertaken in the 18th Dynasty by the pharaoh Akhenaten who decreed that the sun-disc Aten alone should be worshipped. The old divine crew from the solar barque was banished and their temples closed. However, the Egyptian people, and above all their priests, wanted to keep the diversity of their gods and myths, and after Akhenaten's death everything returned to the "divine order", as it was desired by Re in olden times and guaranteed by Maat, the goddess with the feather.

Ra/Re = name of the sun god

On his journey through the underworld the sun god Re takes on various forms, in order to overcome evil. As a "large cat" he cuts up the snake Apophis with his knife.

Painting from the tomb of Nakhtamun, Thebes No. 335, 19th Dynasty

Nut = goddess of the sky *Shu* = god of the air
(with a feather in the name)

The creation of the cosmos, the separation of heaven and earth are shown on the painted sarcophagus of Butehamun, scribe of the necropolis of Thebes. The star-covered body of the sky-goddess is being lifted up by the air-god.
21st Dynasty, Turin, Museo Egizio

The local Theban god Amun, "the hidden one", was elevated to state god and was mostly depicted as a human figure. The air and a breath of wind are his element, indicated by the plumed crown (the feathers have disappeared from this statuette).
From Karnak, 18th Dynasty, slate, height 58 cm, Cairo, Egyptian Museum

The Wild Daughters of the Sun

Many stories were told about the sun-god, which made sense of cosmic events. Each morning the sky, in the shape of a woman, gave birth to Re, every evening she swallowed him again and Re travelled at night through the underworld. The myth of the eye of the sun tells how Hathor-Tefnut, "apple of the eye" and daughter of Re, fled into the desert, infuriated after a disagreement. She stayed away and the sun disappeared until the goddess was brought back by cunning and persuasion to the joy of all. (A story that can well explain the changing of the seasons).

Re once sent his daughter Hathor out as a flaming eye of the sun, to destroy disobedient mankind. When the god, shocked by his dreadful rage, decided to spare some people after all, he resorted to cunning to end the massacre, offering Hathor blood-red beer to drink. She became intoxicated, fell asleep, and so mankind was spared.

The daughter of Re has a dual nature. The Egyptians preferred their feminine divinities to be motherly, gentle beings giving protection and food, but they show her as moody and dangerous. The lion-headed Sakhmet, who as protector goddess of doctors is responsible for medicine, even sent wars and epidemics. Hathor can cause havoc, but as "cow of the sky", lifted the sun-disc over the horizon, suckled the pharaohs with her milk and also gave food and shade in the form of a tree-goddess. The cow-eared goddess was worshipped as the lady of fertility, love, music and dance, although when she left her temple in Dendera each year, and travelled on the Nile to Edfu in order to marry

Hathor, the beautiful daughter of Re, is wearing the sun-disc on her head. In Dendera she was worshipped as the goddess of love, music and dance. However, like most Egyptian deities, she could be wild and dangerous.
Detail from a stone relief on the "birth-house" of Dendera, Roman Period, around 100 A. D.

Hathor = house of Horus

Hathor is wearing the sun-disc on a pair of horns, because one of her incarnations is that of a cow. As "cow of the sky" she lifts the falcon-god Re-Horakhte out of the primeval waters (indicated by a pool of water). In this way she is helping the sun in its rebirth every morning, thus bringing fruitfulness to the land.
Painting from the tomb of Irinufer, Thebes No. 290, Ramesside Period

Hathor also wears the sun-disc on her skin as the lion-headed Sakhmet. "She who is powerful" sends wars and epidemics; however, if she is soothed through prayer, she protects from precisely these ills. The sickly pharaoh Amenhotep III had more than 600 larger-than-life statues of the lion-goddess erected.
Thebes, 18th Dynasty, granite, height 189 cm, Berlin, Egyptian Museum

The tree-goddess, the "lady of the sycamore", is extending her breast to the dead pharaoh. "He is being suckled by his mother Isis" is written under this picture on a column in the coffin chamber of Tuthmosis III. Isis and Hathor, both nursing fertility goddesses, fused over the centuries into a single entity. *Valley of the Kings, 18th Dynasty*

the falcon-headed Horus, it was advisable to make her drunk on the way and soothe her with music.

In the Late Period Hathor fuses with another always well-loved goddess, Isis, who stands at the bow of the solar barque and who once even succeeded in outwitting the sun-god himself. Re had become old and weak, for in Egypt even the gods themselves are subject to the ravages of time. Isis created a poisonous snake by magic, which bit the unwary Re. Only Isis could heal him, but her price was to learn the true, secret name of the sun-god, who so often changed shape and name. To put an end to his pain Re finally agreed. By knowing his name, Isis held the power of the "magic realm" over the once so powerful sun-god.

As "god's mother, lady of the sky, divine adoratrice," the cult of Isis, together with Osiris, spread the furthest in the Late Period. As Isis-Aphrodite she was worshipped throughout the Mediterranean area. By now she was wearing a floaty, Greek garment and a head decoration of ears of corn, cow horns, sun-disc and ostrich plumes.
Ptolemaic, fired clay, height 14.6 cm, University of Leipzig, Egyptian Museum

Isis

Isis is both sister and wife to Osiris, king of the kingdom of the dead, and mother of his son Horus, whom she brought up in hiding, protecting him from his enemies. She was worshipped above all in the temple of Philae as a mother and tutelary god. Her representational feature is the throne which she wears on her head.
Tomb of Horemheb, Valley of the Kings, Thebes, 18th Dynasty

Magic for Love – and for Destruction

The god Bes, protecting spirit of Egyptian houses, whose picture was worn as an amulet by countless Egyptians. The dwarf watched over love, marriage and birth and by his ugliness was supposed to scare away all evil spirits.
From Dendera, Graeco-Roman, sandstone, height 96 cm, Cairo, Egyptian Museum

Heka, the god of magic stands in the solar barque next to the other gods, because magic for the Egyptians was an energy affecting the whole cosmos, an all-pervading ancient force of elemental strength.

The world was created by magic and had to be preserved and protected by magic. It was as much a part of Egyptian religion as medicine and ruled all Egyptian life to a degree unimaginable to us.

It was not practised in secret but quite officially as part of the duties of the priests. Whenever Nubian or Libyan enemies threatened the land for instance, a "proscription spell" was carried out to destroy them; for this the names of the foreign rulers and "all who are loyal to them, heroes, fast-runners and allies" were written on clay jars which were shattered and trodden underfoot. The cursing formula: "may you smash and overcome your enemies and grind them under your shoe!" was even found on a coffin.

In everyday life as well, the Egyptians took refuge in magic, in recommended practices that had been "proven a million times". For example, in the Late Period a certain Sarpamom calls on the demon Antinoos in a papyrus and beseeches him to obtain for him the love of Ptolemais, daughter of Aias (the knowledge of the name, the true identity is also indispensable here): "Bind her, so that she cannot associate with, nor want to have any other man than me. Do not let her eat, drink, love, go out, or be able to sleep except with me, Sarpamon alone! [...] Draw her by the hair, by the innards until I possess her, make her subservient to me for her whole life, so that she loves me, desires me, tells me all her thoughts!" As part of this love magic, without doubt, a small wax figure of the woman or a love potion would also be used as well as the spell, for the "practical", the deed, was always included in the "word".

Over eighty per cent of all magic rituals concerned the everyday sphere, for example helping to ward off colds and fever. For the protection of mother and child there were amulets and written magic spells, which were worn round the neck or could be eaten. Hopes for healing the many snake bites or scorpion stings were pinned on stone slabs, known as "cippi". They show the son of Isis, the Horus child, who is victorious over crocodiles and throttles snakes and scorpions with his bare hands. If water is allowed to run over this stone tablet and then drunk, a share in the protection that Isis grants is bestowed upon her child which will then be healthy.

But the magic was not always effective. Nectanebo II, the last pharaoh of Egyptian blood, (after him Persians and Greeks ascended to the throne) was, according to a later legend, famous as a great magician. He did not need an army, as whenever the Persian enemy threatened his country he made small soldiers and ships out of wax and floated them in a basin full of water. By magical powers these came

Demons such as the crocodile-headed "Swallowing Monster" not only lurked in the underworld. To protect themselves in everyday life, the Egyptians took refuge in magic, consulting magic books. Their writer was considered to be Thoth himself, the god of knowledge and writing with the ibis head. *Detail from the Any papyrus, 18th Dynasty, London, British Museum*

Isis, the "great in magic", is standing at the bow of the divine barque during the nightly journey through the underworld. Together with Heka, the god of magic, she is helping the boat's crew to vanquish the demons. *Drawing in the tomb of Tuthmosis III, Thebes, Valley of the Kings, 18th Dynasty*

alive and drove out the enemy. One day, however, the magic no longer worked and the wax creatures no longer came alive. The Persians occupied Egypt with no resistance and Nectanebo had to flee. His magic had become ineffective, because the Egyptian gods had gone over to the enemy; they had left the land on the Nile for ever.

The Egyptians also hoped for magical help from the son of Isis, the Horus child. Snake and scorpion bites were healed by water that had flowed over his stone image.
Horus stele from Alexandria, Ptolemaic Period, slate, height 14 cm

Demons were summoned to protect newborn infants, and were carved in ivory on the "magic wand": frog, hippopotamus and Aha, who strangled snakes with his bare hands.
Wand amulet, Middle Kingdom, 12th Dynasty, length 36 cm, Cairo, Egyptian Museum

The eye of the gods was omnipresent. Beneficial or threatening,
it accompanied the Egyptians
through life and death.
*Bangle of king Shoshonk I, from
Tanis, 945–924 B. C., cloisonné
work with lapis lazuli, dia-
meter 6.5 cm, Cairo, Egyptian
Museum*

Nectanebo II, the last native
Egyptian pharaoh, before Egypt fell
to the Greeks, is here still under
the protection of Horus. Because
the gods forsook him, he had to
leave his country.
*Statue of Nectanebo, probably from
Heliopolis, 30th Dynasty, 360–343
B. C., height 72 cm, New York,
The Metropolitan Museum of Art,
Rogers Fund, 1934 (34.2.1.)*

Heka = god of magic

Temples were houses for the gods –
if they settled in them, order,
happiness and prosperity reigned in
the land. For this reason each
pharaoh built temples or enlarged
those of his predecessors and placed
his own likeness as a guarding
statue in front of the door.
Luxor temple

Temples –
Where Heaven and Earth Meet

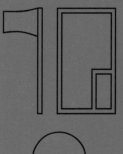

hut-netscher = house of god

The gods of Egypt did not live in a far-away heaven, but here on Earth in mighty temples. Across the whole country the pharaoh built splendid fortified houses in their honour. When the gods accepted them, and entered the inner sanctum of the temple to unite with their statue of gold or silver, then happiness, order and prosperity were ensured. For this reason the country was covered with "houses to the gods", giant complexes which, with their mighty white-washed double towers, stood much higher than any other buildings. Flags fluttered high above them on masts "reaching to the stars". A high wall surrounded the entire sacred part of the temple, which also included a grain store, priests' apartments, a library and a scribes' school, but these utilitarian buildings were made of mud and have long since disappeared. On both sides of the gate were pylons, massive wide towers with sloping outer walls, a symbol for a house of the gods since the 11th Dynasty. The monumentality of these pylons was particularly impressive, as were the enormous reliefs depicting the pharaoh brandishing a club and "vanquishing the enemy" – a motif which was both a deterrent and protection against any danger to the temple and the country. The basic plan of the temples was simple and was used over thousands of years: A straight path led from the gate, down the centre of the temple, through several halls to the chamber in which the cult image of the god stood. This was the heart of the temple, the inner

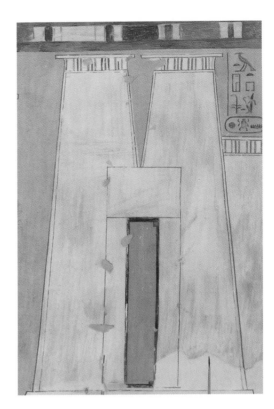

Pylons formed the temple entrance: two wide, massive towers with sloping outer walls.
Wall-painting in the tomb of Amenmessu, Thebes No.19

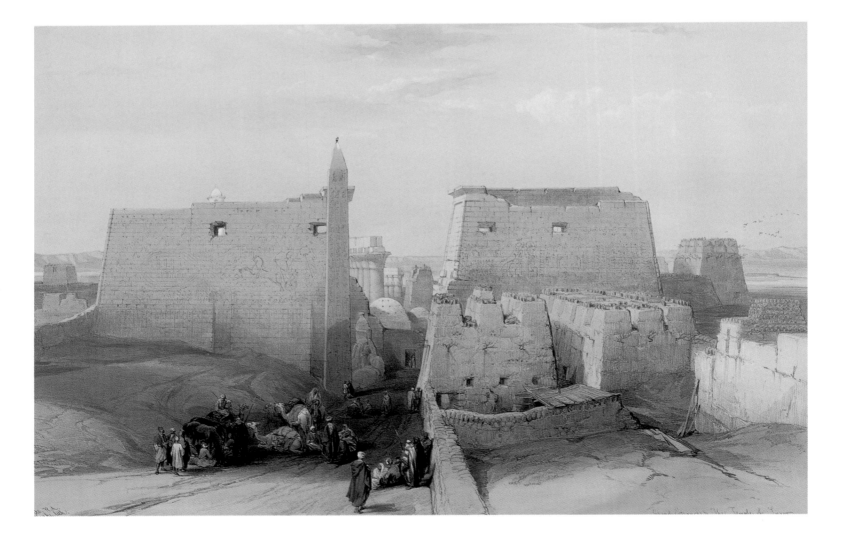

Sphinxes guard the path to the temple, through which the statues of the gods were carried. In parallel rows they border the axis which led into the temple through gates, courtyards and hypostyle halls. *Avenue of sphinxes in front of the 1st pylon of the Luxor temple*

The temples towered like mighty fortresses, their very size making them impressive. The English painter David Roberts recorded the condition of the Luxor temple in 1838. *London, Victoria and Albert Museum*

sanctum, located on the central axis at the furthest point from the entrance.

Between the entrance and the inner sanctum were the halls, only the first of which, a courtyard open to the skies and located directly behind the pylons, was accessible to ordinary people on special feast days. Next in sequence came a giant, dimly lit columned hall, closed off to ordinary people. This hall led to the room with the sacrificial table, and the barque room beyond (in processions the image of the god was carried on the barque by priests). Finally came the closed inner sanctum, the holy of holies. This basic layout was also used by kings for their own mortuary temples, which from the Middle Kingdom onwards, were dedicated to at least one god as well as to the dead pharaoh. For all its monumentality, such an ensemble still managed to give an impression of harmony. The clarity, order and symmetry of these temples can be seen today in the Ptolemaic temple complexes of Edfu, Philae and Dendera.

If a pharaoh wanted to enlarge the temple of a predecessor, he either built the whole thing anew, or he added a second columned hall, an open courtyard and another pair of pylons in front of the old forecourt. In the New Kingdom long processional paths led up to the temple, always in line with the central axis and bordered with trees or sphinxes (a creature made up of a lion's body and the head of a ram

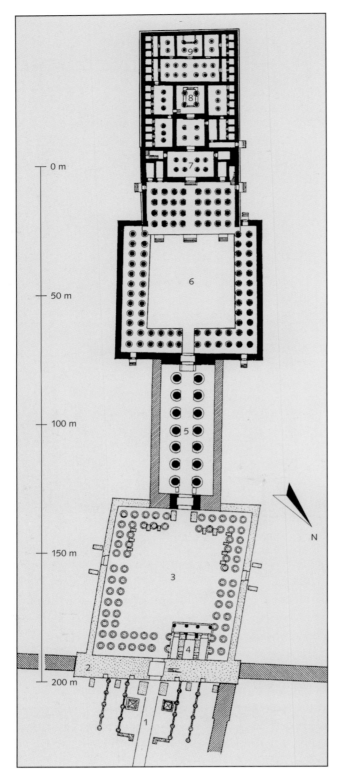

The different construction phases can be seen on the plan of the Luxor temple, started by Amenhotep III, and developed by Ramesses II.

1. Forecourt with obelisks and colossi statues
2. Pylon
3. Court of Ramesses II.
4. Temple of Tuthmosis III.
5. Colonnade of Amenhotep III.
6. Court of Amenhotep III.
7. Hypostyle hall
8. Barque shrine
9. Sanctuary

The pharaoh and the goddess of writing and measurement, Seshat, marking the boundaries of the grounds of a new temple with a rope. This symbolic ceremony for laying foundations was called "stretching of the rope". Here Queen Hatshepsut is depicted as the male partner of the goddess. *Block of relief from the so-called "Red Chapel" of Hatshepsut at Karnak*

or human being). The path ran down to the landing stage on the Nile. This is how the extensive complex at Karnak was created. Through continual extension in the 18th Dynasty the modest Amun temple of Sesostris I grew into the giant temple complex of the god of the empire with ten pairs of pylons, a hall filled with 134 closely spaced columns and over one thousand sphinxes. The main axis was always east-west, running towards the Nile, with the front of the temple, wherever possible actually facing the river. Books of rules set out the proportions, the favoured unit of measurement being the cubit, in multiples of ten. The Great Hall of Karnak, for example, measures 200 x 100 cubits (1 cubit = 52.3 centime-tres). The pharaoh himself decided, in a ceremonial ritual, what the outline of the temple should be; together with Seshat, the goddess of measurements, he stretched out the marker string. We are not told who drew up the plans and carried out the work; the only name inscribed for all time in the stone walls is that of the pharaoh for whom it was built, not that of his architect.

The hypostyle hall of the temple of Karnak around 1850, taken by the Frenchman Maxime Du Camp, who was the first to photograph the Egyptian monuments for scientific purposes. Many of the columns have now been re-erected and restored.

Mounds Rising up out of the Floods

The myth of the "primeval mound" rising up out of the floods played a role in designing not only pyramids, but also temples. Details from temple architecture and decoration underline the symbolism of the building as an island rising out of the waters. On the mighty wall surrounding the temple complex at Dendera, for example, the line of joints between the various layers of bricks is not horizontal, but wavy, to indicate the "waves of the primeval ocean". The ocean was believed to be directly below the temple, its water feeding the "holy lake" and the springs at which the priests washed themselves before being allowed to enter the sanctuary.

The floor of the temple (mostly black like the mud from the Nile) rises from room to room; the priests had to carry the image of the god up ramps. There it stood, enclosed within a shrine at the highest point, the shrine's pyramid-shaped roof, carved from a large block of hard granite or basalt, also being an abstract representation of the primeval mound. Nowadays most of the cult images of gold or silver have disappeared, but their solid shrines are still standing, sometimes isolated amidst the ruins.

The image of the god was carried in processions on a barque. In the columned halls it must have seemed as if it were floating on the water of the primeval ocean. For the decorated columns resembled bundles of papyrus or lotus

According to an old picture, temples grew up like hills out of the waters. In the 20th century when the dams of Aswan had been built, many temples were under threat from the water. To save the complex of Philae, in 1980 UNESCO moved it and set it on higher ground. *Temple of Isis on the island of Philae, on the Nubian border, Ptolemaic Period*

The bricks of the wall surrounding the Hathor temple of Dendera are laid in a wave formation – this is also a reminder of the primeval ocean, which is believed to lie under all temples. *Roman Imperial Period, 100–200 A. D.*

The most robust element in a temple was the divine shrine. It alone towers out of the rubble, which is all that remains of the temple complex of Mendes (Nile Delta).
26th Dynasty, red granite, height 8 m

plants, shooting up out of the "mud" and turning the halls into an imaginary forest of flowers. In Karnak the two plants which were the symbols of upper and lower Egypt, the lotus and the papyrus, decorate the top of two particularly beautiful granite pillars in front of the barque room. They can be seen today towering up out of the surrounding ruins. When they were first raised, they symbolically held up the two halves of the country above the head of the pharaoh as he stepped into the shrine.

The ceilings, now partly collapsed, were once painted blue and decorated with stars; giant falcons stretched out their wings over the doors and the goddess of heaven, Nut, arched her snake-like naked body over the earth. The entire cosmos was depicted in the temple, complete with water, earth and sky.

In front of the temple gates stood monumental statues of rulers and pairs of obelisks, some 32 metres high. They were made of red granite from the quarries of Aswan and weighed

In the Amun temple of Karnak 134 columns are topped by opened or closed lotus blossoms, like plants that grew out of the primeval mud. *Hypostyle hall, 19th Dynasty*

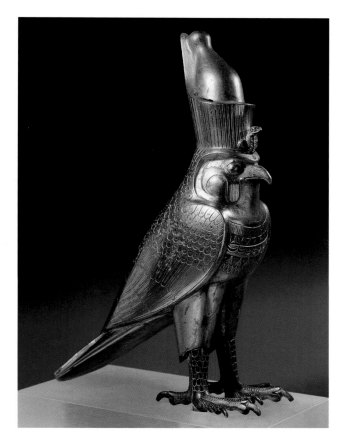

Cleaned, anointed and treated with incense daily – the silver cult image of the Horus falcon was pampered so that the gods might graciously settle down in it.
Provenance unknown,
27th Dynasty, height 26.9 cm,
Munich, State collection
of Egyptian art

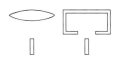

raper = shrine

The pyramid-shaped roof of the divine shrine in the Horus temple of Edfu was also supposed to evoke the primeval mound. It stands at the end of the long, ascending path through the temple in a dark chamber, the permanently sealed "sanctuary".
30th Dynasty

over 450 tons. Light reflected from the gilded bronze cladding on the pyramid-shaped tip of the obelisks. They are interpreted as symbols of the sun, a type of physical representation of a ray of sunlight. They, too, despite their elegant needle-like shape, probably derive from an ancient, irregularly shaped sacred stone from Heliopolis, the Benben Stone, which is again a representation of the primeval mound.

The temple interior was brightly painted, but today only traces remain. 19th century painters attempted to reproduce the original condition.
Hypostyle hall of the temple of Isis at Philae

The obelisks were made from red granite and were up to 32 m high – an Egyptian invention and, like the pyramids, much exported and imitated. With their gilded tops they were considered to be rays of sunlight turned into stone.
Obelisk of Tuthmosis I, Karnak, 18th Dynasty

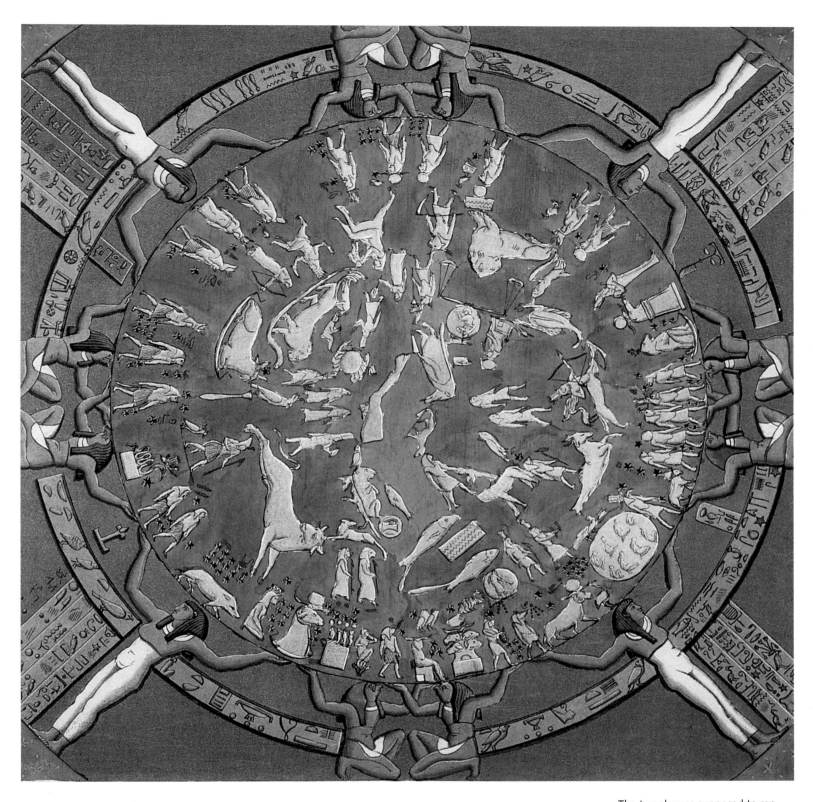

The temple was supposed to represent the entire cosmos. On the ceiling was the night sky, supported by gods, painted with constellations. Some of the Egyptian signs of the zodiac are known to us today. *Astronomical sky chart from the temple of Hathor in Dendera, original now in the Louvre, re-drawn by Domenico Valeriano in 1835*

pet = sky

Gods and Cult Worship

"May you awake in peace!" is how the priest greeted the divine image of Amun in the mornings. Thus is it described in the "Morning Song for Festival Days" on a papyrus from the temple library of Karnak, found in an antique shop in 1845 by the Berlin Egyptologist Richard Lepsius.

This exhortation to the "Lord of Fertility" was intended to put him in a favourable mood, for gods could be terrible indeed, as indicated by the uraeus on their foreheads.

Since the fate of Egypt was dependent on Amun, he and the other gods had to have all their needs taken care of. And so each morning, in all the temples of the land, a complicated ritual took place.

The priest performing the ceremony lit a flare on entering the innermost, dark, windowless chamber in the temple, then he broke the seal on the door to the inner sanctum and presented himself to the cult image of the god: "Truly, I am a servant of god [...] the king is the one [...] who sends me to look at the god. I am come to do what may be done."

And there was much indeed to do: Incense was burned to assuage the dangerously arching serpent on the diadem of the god; the shrine had to be cleaned, and the statue had to have fresh make-up, be cleaned with water and incense, redressed, crowned and anointed with ten different oils. Finally it was then magically reawakened through the "mouth opening", closed up again in its shrine and the door sealed. After he had carefully removed all traces of his own footsteps on the floor and extinguished the flare, the priest left the holy of holies until the following day. The only person actually permitted to perform these rituals was in fact the pharaoh himself, but he himself only

Large sections of the temple walls were decorated with sacrificial scenes, such as here in the Red Chapel of Hatshepsut. This building was destroyed by her successors, but the blocks were used in the walls of other buildings, so that it was possible to find them again.
In the left-hand scene, milk is being offered to Amun-Re. In the right-hand scene Hatshepsut is offering unguents to the falcon-headed Horus.

senetscher = incense

Even gods need food. The kneeling King Nectanebo I is offering a conically shaped loaf of bread as a sacrifice. In reality, the daily ritual in the numerous temples was not carried out by the pharaoh, but by priests as part of their duty.
Detail from a relief in the temple of Nectanebo I, Alexandria, 30th Dynasty, London, British Museum

Like the Egyptians, their gods loved the fragrance of incense above all else. Carefully Prince Amunherke-peshef, son of Ramesses III, throws incense into the pan of a lavishly worked incense burner.
Wall-painting in the tomb of Prince Amunherkepeshef, son of Ramesses III, 20th Dynasty, Thebes, Valley of the Queens

attended on feast days and allowed priests to carry out these duties for him in the many temples of the land. On the walls of the temples, however, on which the ritual was presented in colour relief, the king acts alone: he is the one praying, burning incense, making sacrifices, bringing gifts, water, milk or wine, for gods, too, needed nourishment. In return for these gifts, the gods give the king the cross with a handle, the *ankh*, symbol of life, or the "good" sceptre: "I give you life, goodness and health ever more," say the hieroglyphs. In another scene the pharaoh is depicted handing the god a small statue, Maat with a feather on her head. Maat symbolises justice and order.

The ritual served to prevent chaos and disorder. If it was forgotten, or if the pharaoh or priests neglected their duties, then the gods would be angry and leave the land, no longer "full of temples", but "full of tombs and corpses". And, they were warned, "The earth will turn like a potter's wheel [...] the river full of blood [...] mourning will spread across the land, mixed with wailing. All people, large and small, will wish they were dead!"

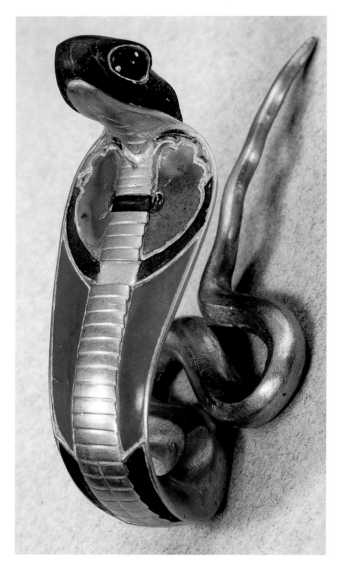

The uraeus destroys all enemies by spewing fire. It protects the pharaoh and rears threateningly from the head-dress of the gods. It must be soothed time and again in a daily ritual.
Probably part of a crown of Sesostris II, Middle Kingdom, 12th Dynasty, solid gold, head of lapis lazuli, eye made of granite, height 6.7 cm, Cairo, Egyptian Museum

In exchange for their sacrificial offerings, the gods gave gifts to men, especially the "cross with a handle", simultaneously symbol and hieroglyph for "*ankh*", that is "life". Since "*ankh*" also means "mirror", an expensive mirror-case of Tutankhamun's takes the shape of the cross with a handle. The mirror from inside was probably stolen by tomb robbers.
Mirror-case, 18th Dynasty, wood with gold, silver plate, semi-precious stones and glass, height 27 cm, Cairo, Egyptian Museum

In her left hand the goddess is holding the life-giving *ankh*, in her right hand a long staff with a strange animal head – the *Uas* sceptre, sign of her power. King Horemheb is bringing her wine in bulbous vessels.
Relief scene in the tomb of King Horemheb, Thebes, Valley of the Kings, 18th Dynasty

Incense and Myrrh

Egyptologists have described Egyptian temples as a kind of magic "machine" designed to preserve the world order. Egyptians themselves used the term "horizon". This word described not only a geographical location, but also a religious one: Heaven and earth, this world and the next, meet at the point where the temple stands. The scribe Iahemes thought that "the sky itself seemed to be in the temple when the sun rose".

These words were inscribed in the 18th Dynasty on the outer wall of the mortuary temple of King Djoser; Iahemes was therefore admiring a cult place which was already over 1000 years old. No one is sure if he actually entered the temple, for ordinary people generally did not have access. Unlike the cathedrals of the Middle Ages, temples in Ancient Egypt were not designed for worship by the mass of believers. Public access was only granted on certain occasions, and then only to the forecourt. Reliable records about the craftsmen of Deir el-Medinah, the builders of the pharaohs' tombs near Thebes and of simple ordinary folk, show that they preferred their own local deities to the gods of the empire. In small village shrines or at altars in private households, they worshipped for example the patron saint Merserger, the "friend of quiet" who lived in snake form near the top of a mountain. They prayed to her for protection. Men with a higher status in society could gain access to the outer buildings in the temple complexes. For, in contrast to the official priests who were either appointed directly by the pharaoh or who inherited their office, the lower-ranking lay priests carried out their duties for just a few months and were then replaced. Thus

a considerable number of men were able to participate in the glory and economic benefits of these rich institutions. Priests can be recognised in depictions by their simple long aprons and closely shorn heads. "They shave off all their body hair every two days," reports Herodotus, "so that no louse or other pest can attach itself to the servants of god [...] Twice a day and twice at night they bathe in cold water." They were called "the pure ones" and were permitted, for example, to carry the statue of the god when it was brought out into the light on feast days. Amun, in his 80-metre-long god's barque, was carried on the shoulders of 30 priests from Karnak to Luxor, via the processional route, or to the landing stage on the Nile. En route he rested in pavilions known as "barque stations" and gave the people a chance to cheer him from afar.

Ordinary people could turn to a mediator to gain the ear of a god. "Come to me! I will pass on all messages to Amun in Thebes [...] For I am the herald whom the king has appointed to hear the prayers of the common man" was the wording on the base of a statue at the entrance to the Amun temple of Amenhotep III. Requests or thanks, each bearing the originator's name, were written on statuettes or small stone tablets, the latter often decorated with the ear of the god for whom the message was intended. The believers deposited them in the temple courtyard. In a pit near Karnak over 17,000 such stelae were found.

These modest plaques are the only record of the piousness of ordinary people; the representations on the inner walls of the temples tell us nothing about their beliefs. However, sometimes we see, carved on the back wall of the inner sanctum, pictures of ears, to which ordinary folk could turn with their prayers. Alternatively, like the good devout

dua = worshipping

State gods were responsible for kings, while the ordinary people took their everyday worries to local deities. In the village of Deir el-Medinah a snake goddess was worshipped. Paneb's three sons are praying to her on a stele. *Stele of Paneb, 19th Dynasty, London, British Museum*

The state gods only came out of their sanctuaries on special feast days. Shaven-headed priests carried them through the temple area in a sealed shrine on a barque.
Relief at the Red Chapel of Hatshepsut in Karnak

The divine barque was sometimes set down during processions in Karnak, e. g. in the "White chapel", which was erected by Sesostris I during the 12th Dynasty. It was also destroyed, but was rebuilt from the remaining unbroken stones.

Iahemes, they could write their wishes directly on the walls as graffiti. Wishes such as: "May heaven rain fresh myrrh, may it drip with incense."

The well-maintained temples of the Late Period bear witness to three thousand years' refinement of religious architecture. The god Horus as a heavenly falcon is still on guard in front of the façade of the temple of Edfu in Upper Egypt, crowned with the pharaohs' double crown. *Ptolemaic Period*

The craftsman Bay from Deir el-Medinah appeals directly to the ear of God, having three pairs of ears depicted on his stele, for "the listening god comes to those who call him," says a hymn, "he is radiant in his appearances, rich in ears."
Stele, dedicated to Amun (depicted as a ram), in Deir el-Medinah, found in the grounds of the temple of Hathor, 19th–20th Dynasty, limestone, height 24.5 cm

The statue of Amenhotep, son of Hapu, a high official, stands at the gate of the 10th pylon in the temple of Karnak. The text on the base reports his deeds in which he offers to act as mediator sending the temple visitor's prayers to Amun-Re.
Karnak, 18th Dynasty, granite, height 128 cm

Tomb Robbers and Curses

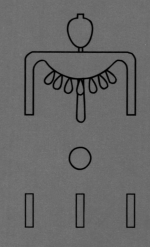

hedsch = silver, money

For many well-off Egyptians, the desire to rest in peace after death was not fulfilled. Robbers forced their way into their tombs and took out anything of value. That happened mostly in periods with no strong central power, in the Intermediate Periods. The oldest indication of a robbery dates from the years after the breakdown of the Old Kingdom. King Merikare (approximately 2100 B.C.) informed his son, "there were battles at the burial grounds and the tombs were plundered. I joined in myself." About a thousand years later (1121 B.C.) Ramesses IX ordered the necropolises in western Thebes to be examined. His officials found that a royal tomb and many private graves had been broken into. The confessions of the robbers have been preserved. "We took our copper tools and cut a way into the pyramid tomb of the king [...] we discovered his subterranean chamber and climbed down, flaming torches in our hands [...] and we found the queen's tomb·[...] we opened the (outer) sarcophagi and the (inner) coffins in which they lay, and found the venerable mummy of the king, equipped with a crescent-shaped sword. Numerous amulets and gold jewellery lay around his neck. He was wearing

a gold mask. The venerable mummy of the king was completely covered with gold. His coffins were decorated with gold inside and out and inlaid with every kind of precious stone. We ripped the gold off [...] we found the queen in exactly the same way and we ripped everything off again [...] and set fire to their coffins."

Over the millennia most of the tombs have been broken into and robbed. When the archaeologists came the burial chambers looked like these (left) in the necropolis of Douch in the Charga oasis.

Whether they were Egyptians from pharaonic times, or Mohammedan or Christian visitors – they all opened burial chambers and plundered them. The Frenchman Jean de Thevenot was one of the first Europeans to have coffins broken open and to report on the findings. His report complete with engravings "Voyage au Levant" appeared in 1664.

Economic Effects

The tomb robberies assumed such proportions in the following centuries that in 950 King Siamun gathered together all the mummies of kings and hid them at Deir el-Bahari to protect them. In 1871 A.D., the famous communal tomb, known as the "cachette" (French for 'hiding-place') was discovered by tomb robbers and plundered. Ten years later, the Egyptian Antiquities Service brought the royal remains to safety in the newly founded Cairo Museum. In times of need, presumably all necropolises were ransacked, producing quite extraordinary profits from the funerary objects stolen from them. This had repercussions on the economy. In good times royal economic planners distributed the basic foodstuffs, while in bad times, that is those in which the central power was weak, the supply system broke down and craftsmen and workers had to find bread, oil and beer for themselves. Quite a few then helped themselves from the tombs. The profits of the robbers and those who received the stolen goods were often far in excess of what was needed to relieve hunger. Occasionally it

corresponded to several years' income and there was no opportunity to invest it profitably. There were no banks and most of the land belonged to the king, his officials or the temples. Therefore the profits were spent, so even craftsmen bought slaves, ate beef and drank sweetened wine. The short-term wealth also forced up food prices and many people who had not been involved in the plunder could not afford to pay them.

Tomb robbery thus made the economic chaos worse, although some Egyptologists maintain that it had highly positive economic effects. They argue that through the distinctive Egyptian cult of the underworld, a hefty part of the people's wealth went underground and stayed there unused – the thieves brought it back into circulation and so, in a criminal way, rendered a service to the national economy.

The lady wearing the apron, Margaret Murray, was one of the first female Egyptologists and was employed by the Museum of Manchester. In 1907 she was photographed at the undressing of a mummy.

18th century pharmaceutical pot for "mummiya", a powder that had been sent to Europe since the Middle Ages for its alleged great healing powers.

The Trade in Mummies

The Arabs, who ruled Egypt from 640 B.C., had little respect for the Egyptian cult of the dead. Their tomb robbers had written instructions, e.g. the "Book of the Lost Pearls". "Go north-west from the pyramid and you will come to a white mountain. At its foot a path leads to a valley where the ground is soft. Light a smoking fire with tar, liquid styrax and wool from a black sheep" and the magic fire will point the way to the gold.

The trade in mummies was relatively late in developing. Permission was given for the first intact body to be transported to Europe in 1600; in 1615 two came to Rome from Saqqara and then in 1728 from Rome to the Dresden Curiosities Cabinet of Augustus the Strong.

But there was interest even earlier, not in bodies, but in a powder called "mummiya", a word taken from the Persian. It describes a natural bitumen, a blackish asphalt, allegedly with great healing powers. Persian kings used to present European rulers with small portions of the valuable mineral substance, thereby arousing curiosity and needs that could only be satisfied with substitute materials. An Arab doctor suggested, as a substitute, pine resin which had been used in embalming and had become associated with the bodies. So it came about that the deceased, whom the Egyptians had prepared for eternity, were called mummies and, from the late Middle Ages, business-minded traders ensured that it was shipped in powder form from Alexandria to European ports. The French king François I (1494–1547) is said to have always carried a small packet of "mummiya" with him to treat wounds, and until well into the 19th century there was a pot of "mummiya" in every good apothecary. As late as 1924, "mumia vera Aegyptica" was on the price list of the pharmaceutical company E. Merck in Darmstadt. Price per kilo: 12 gold marks.

The interest in intact mummies arose after Napoleon and his scientists had made Egypt popular in 1798 – tourists regarded a mummy as an appropriate souvenir. At home, they either placed it in their own rarities room, donated it to a museum or unwrapped it. This mummy undressing was sometimes turned into a social event. A Lord Londesborough announced the following on printed cards on 10th June 1850 in his London home: "A mummy from Thebes to be unrolled at half-past two." In 1883, the Prussian prince Friedrich-Karl brought a mummy back to Berlin from his travels in Egypt, and had it unwrapped on his billiard table. An interested group of people with limited means founded a mummy association in the Westphalian town of Hamm and had a specimen sent to them. What sensitive participants in the mummy organisations felt is outlined by Théophile Gautier, the French poet. The occasion was an undressing in Paris during the World Exhibition of 1867. "… two white eyes with large black pupils flashed with artificial life between brownish eyelids. They were enamel eyes […] This sparkling, stiff stare in a dead face made an eerie impression. To the living, who gathered frantically around it, the body appeared to be observing them with scornful astonishment." Giovanni Belzoni, an Italian adventurer, who in 1817 was commissioned by the English consulate to search through rock-cut tombs, gives us a different perspective. In one of the tombs he was feeling his way towards somewhere to sit by faint torchlight: "But when my weight came down on the body of an Egyptian it compressed like a hatbox. Naturally I put out my hands to help support my weight, but to no avail; so I sank right down between broken mummies in a confusion of bones, rags, wooden boxes, which threw up such a lot of dust that for a quarter of an hour I was unable to move […]."

The later history of the mummies is full of macabre details. When in 1881 on the Nile the dead kings were brought out

of the "cachette", they had to go through customs, like all goods imported to Cairo. Mummies were not on the lists of the customs officers, so the official plumped for the nearest equivalent, the tax on dried fish.

The unwrapping of a mummy as a social event at the London residence of Lord Londesborough – a meeting of two cultures. The precision of the day and time seems particularly noteworthy, in view of the thousands of years that the body had lain peacefully hidden away.

Obtaining intact mummies was complicated and expensive, and those who could not afford to have it done privately founded an association. At least that is what some inhabitants of the Westphalian town of Hamm did. Each share in the association cost DM 20 and in 1886 the mummy could be viewed in a restaurant for an entrance fee.

Science versus Dignity

It has long been disputed how far it is consistent with the dignity of the deceased, whether a king or a commoner, to expose them to the stares of a curious public. In practice, the question is mostly decided in conjunction with other interests. This is clearly demonstrated in the case of the Cairo Museum. The famous kings had been exhibited since the end of the last century, but President Sadat had the Room of the Royal Mummies closed, as the newly won self-esteem of the Egyptians was, for him, incompatible with displaying their former rulers. When, in 1994, tourists were excluded owing to threats from Islamic fundamentalists, some of the royal mummies were brought out again. The need for foreign currency overcame any scruples. An example of the most solemn dealings with the dead pharaohs was the reception of the remains of Ramesses II in 1976 in Paris. He was greeted like a guest of state at the airport and 102 scientists were involved in attending to the royal welfare in the Musée de l'Homme. The physical remains were suffering from increasingly serious signs of decay and a fungus, daedalea biennis fries, was identified as the cause. The antidote, gamma rays of cobalt-60, was tested first on minute tissue parts, then on a test mummy: They killed the fungus without damaging the body. Ramesses stayed in Paris for seven months, being measured, X-rayed, analysed in optical slices with the aid of computer tomography and joined together again in three-dimensional images. This revealed a battle wound on his shoulder and a small animal bone in his nose as an embalming aid: his spine was so badly curved that the embalmer must have had to break the cervical vertebrae in order to place the head correctly in the coffin. The Louvre donated an antique piece of linen to cover the body up again when they had finished. The doctors, wrote a reporter, had done the same as the embalming priest, i.e. preserved the body, so that it could be united with its soul.

The Curse of the Pharaohs

During the examination of Ramesses II, all participants had worn mouth and nasal protection – previously doctors had ascertained that fungal cultures on mummies posed dangers to health, particularly for people with weak lungs. Was this the infamous curse of the pharaohs?

For Ancient Egyptians the curse was based on the idea that the dead live again and can intervene in this life. "I will seize his neck like that of a goose" is written on one tomb inscription – the deceased is threatening those who want to do "evil" to his tomb. He will wring his neck and "I will exterminate those he leaves behind, I will ensure that their farms are deserted."

Such threats were not taken seriously by the tomb robbers, but continued to have a deterring effect on the general populace. A report from the 10th century A.D., during the period of Islamic rule, tells of some young men who penetrated Cheops' Pyramid: "They climbed down the slippery path, where they saw bats the size of eagles which flew into their faces [...]." One of them climbed up a shaft, held by a rope. Suddenly, the ground closed over him. "They did their best to pull him out, but their strength was fading [...] they heard a terrifying sound and lost consciousness." When they came round, they left the pyramid and "suddenly their companion appeared out of the earth alive before them, speaking words which were incomprehensible to them, then he fell down dead." A man from Upper Egypt translated the strange words: "In such a way will all those be punished, who strive after that which is not theirs." This punishment is also said to have overtaken Lord Carnarvon, who, due to poor health, lived in the dry heat of Egypt. He financed the discovery of the tomb of Tutankhamun, was present at its opening in 1923 – and died four months later. And that is not all. On the day the tomb was opened, a cobra ate his canary, and at the hour of his death the lights went out in Cairo. Now, it is not a strange occurrence for snakes to eat pets and the electricity plants to stop the power supply in Cairo, but remembering the "curse of the pharaohs", people imbued the two events with great significance. In books and films, which play on people's pleasure in horror, this curse lives on as an Egyptian legacy of a very special sort.

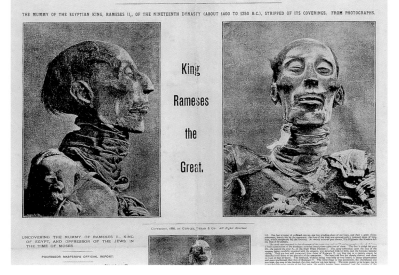

In 1881 several royal mummies, including that of Ramesses II, were discovered in a tomb at Deir el-Bahari, the "cachette", and taken to Cairo. It is pure speculation that Ramesses II may have been the Egyptian ruler who oppressed the people of Israel at the time of Moses, a theory used for advertising by a Boston bookshop in 1887.

No other Egyptian mummy can have been so thoroughly examined, X-rayed and photographed from all angles as that of the great Ramesses. It was almost falling apart and in 1976 was flown to Paris, where scientists identified a fungus which they removed. As well as discovering wounds, tooth decay and an embalming aid in his nose, they also found that in his old age the king had dyed his red hair with henna.

Egypt at a glance, fitted into
a framework which makes the
European perspective very clear.
The Napoleonic N is at the bottom
centre under the emperor's throne.
This engraving comes at the
beginning of the "Description de
l'Égypte", the first scientific
description of the monuments,
the people and the landscape of
Egypt. In 1809 the 20 volumes
began to appear – a happy
outcome of Napoleon's
failed military expedition.

Egypt and
the Western World

Kemet = black earth, Egypt

It is said that the fire in the library at Alexandria destroyed 700,000 papers, important documents of the pharaonic culture, amongst which was the only complete specimen of the king list, written by the priest Manetho.

The library fire is regarded as the end of Ancient Egyptian records, although no one knows exactly when the catastrophe occurred. It may have been in the year 48 B.C., when Caesar ordered the Egyptian fleet to be burned and the flames are said to have spread to the famous temple library. It could also have happened in the year 391 A.D. as the Roman Emperor Theodosius tried to enforce the Christian faith as the state religion and plundered the non-Christian temples. According to a third version, the manuscripts – or what was left of them – were not burned until the 7th century under the rule of the caliphs. It is possible that all three fires occurred. In the case of highly flammable materials like papyrus this seems the most likely cause of their destruction. However, it is also possible that they were destroyed in the imagination of later generations rather than in reality, subsequent generations preferring to see the end of a great tradition shrouded in mystery as a spectacular event, rather than the result of a gradual process over many centuries.

This process came about as the Ancient Egyptian beliefs began to die out, confronting the aggressive dissemination of Christianity, and later the Islamic faith. In Ancient Egypt, spiritual life was closely bound to the temple and once the temple priests were no longer authorised by the pharaoh or supported by the local rulers and the population, their material foundation dwindled away. The priests died with no trained successors and with them died the ability to interpret the hieroglyphs and other Ancient Egyptian scripts. It was not then the flames that ultimately brought about the end, but the decline of religion.

After the death of Cleopatra, Egypt became a Roman province and the former state religion lost its meaning, the gods disappearing with the priests. One of the few exceptions was Isis, whose cult spread all over the Mediterranean. The Isis sculpture originating from around 150 A.D. is carrying a pot in her left hand for the holy water from the Nile. A ship with Nile water was believed to have sailed from Alexandria for Rome every week.

Obelisks were up to 30 metres high, and despite their size several of them were transported to Europe. To the Egyptians the obelisk was considered a shaft of light of the sun god. In Rome a cross was added to the heathen monument by the church.
Copper engraving by Giambattista, Piranesi, 1759

A Secret Inheritance

The Isis cult which originated in Egypt prevailed in Italy, particularly in Rome, for some considerable time, the fascination being further promoted by the presence of Egyptian monuments. Rulers were buried under pyramids and in 10 B.C. the Emperor Augustus had the first obelisk brought to Rome, which can be seen today on the Piazza del Popolo. Another stands in front of St Peter's Cathedral, although the top is adorned by a cross as a clearly visible sign of the supremacy of Christianity over all other religions. However, the cross on top of the obelisk can also be interpreted in a different manner – that Christian teaching

is based on Egypt, with many of the pictures and stories used in the Bible originating from the Nile. There are further similarities: the Egyptians believed, as the Old Testament states, that man was formed out of clay by a God, the Christian concept of hell is similar to the Egyptian underworld with its punishments and dangers, and the pharaohs were going to heaven before Christ was born. The teachings of death and resurrection symbolised for the Egyptian the myth of the dismembered Osiris who was joined back together by Isis: Isis was seen as the protective mother deity, in much the same way that Catholics worship Mary. Also striking are similarities in the manifestations of God – Christ as a lamb or the Holy Ghost as a dove correspond to the Egyptian

tradition according to which their gods appear in animal form and, remarkably, the Holy Trinity of God the Father, the Son and the Holy Ghost is typical of Egyptian thinking – all their gods have more than one manifestation, are interwoven, and very frequently appear in a trinity.

Even events which to us seem inextricably linked with the biblical Christmas story had already taken place a long time before in Egypt. For instance, the story of the pregnant goddess Isis, searching for a guest house being rejected by several fine ladies before finding shelter in the humble hut of a "marsh maiden". Or that of Cheops who (like King Herod) wishes to have three boys killed because it has been predicted that they will become rulers. With regard to the visual symbols, the Coptic cross, the cross of the Egyptian Christians, is derived directly from the *ankh*, the Egyptian symbol for "life".

We could continue the list ad infinitum. While these examples do not call the core statements of Christian dogma into question, they do query the idea nurtured by the Church that all biblical texts come directly from God. For, as religious historians have known for some time, these stories reflect

a strong Egyptian heritage through which, without believers being aware of it, ideas of the heathen pharaonic culture remain alive to this day.

The Egyptians also invented the calendar and divided the day into 24 hours, the year into 365 days, solved certain mathematical problems and drew up lists of illnesses and their remedies: knowledge which was passed on via the Greeks and the Romans and further developed. Just as important, however, to this day, is the example set by the goddess Maat of how people should live together. She symbolises justice, to which all people are committed, and should be of the highest priority for kings. Maat taught that justice must be administered independently of the office of power. In Europe, this goddess lives on in the figure of justice. In western democracies, justice has become the third independent state power along with government and parliament – but the Egyptians thought of it first.

Alchemy can also be traced back to the Egyptians. One of their aims was to find an elixir which could bestow eternal life. Behind this desire for immortality lies the Egyptian idea of the preservation of the body in the underworld, which is

21st July 1798: Recognisable from afar on his white horse, Napoleon leads the French troops against the Mameluke cavalry. One of those taking part, the officer and painter Louis François Lejeune, glorified the encounter in a large-scale battle panorama. The "Battle at the Pyramids" and other skirmishes were won, but the expedition corps was lost when the English burnt the French ships.
1806, oil on canvas, 180 x 258 cm, Palace of Versailles

Napoleon and Baron Denon

For many centuries, Europeans knew no more about Egypt than what they had read in the Bible: The story of Joseph who overcame bad harvest years through clever stockpiling, or the tale of Moses who led the people of Israel out of Egypt. And of course, it was also at the Nile that Joseph and Mary were forced to flee Herod's murderous troops with the baby Jesus.

An active interest in this distant country and its culture was not awakened until the renaissance, after which it became hugely fashionable for all levels of educated society in the 18th century, reaching its peak after the landing of Napoleon in Alexandria on 1 July 1798. He brought 35,000 soldiers with him intending to break English supremacy in the Near East, only to suffer a crushing defeat by the English troops. However, Napoleon had more than 100 artists, technicians, geographers and architects in his expedition corps, with an average age of around twenty-five. While on the one hand they were supposed to help set up a future French colony, they were also to carry out as intensive an investigation as possible into the country and its cultural monuments. Under the protection of the soldiers, they therefore measured pyramids, temples, obelisks and made records of buildings and works of art. In 1802, one of the Frenchmen, Baron Vivant Denon, published a travel journal of his experiences, which ran to 40 editions, was translated into German and English and became the forerunner of the science now known as Egyptology. Appointed by Napoleon as president of all French museums, Denon founded the "Musée Napoléon", now the Louvre, a wing of which has been named after him. A second result of this expedition was a joint work published under the title "Description de l'Egypte". Comprising 20 volumes, this work is a unique undertaking of its time in both scope and accuracy, recording inhabitants, animals, plants and landscapes as well as descriptions of monuments from the past. The fact that these scholars occasionally "restored" a temple on paper, i.e. showed it in its hypothetical original state, or invented a Nile bridge which never existed, does not detract from the scientific value of their work. It was published between 1809 and 1828 and is still used as a first-class source of reference to this day, particularly for those monuments which have since been destroyed.

then re-animated by the soul. Several of the alchemic symbols are also Egyptian: the snake biting its own tail symbolises eternity and the phoenix rising from the ashes represents the resurrection. Alexandria is regarded as the birthplace of alchemy, and the Greek God Hermes Trismegistus is revered as its inventor. The Egyptian equivalent is Thoth, the god of wisdom and writing, and leader of souls through the underworld. Modern chemistry was developed from the experiments and techniques of the alchemists, and the name still reminds us of its origins: "Kemet" is Ancient Egyptian for "black earth", the black country, the fertile land of the Nile after which the Egyptians named their state.

Jean François Champollion succeeded in deciphering Egyptian script. In his "Grammaire égyptienne" he also deals with colours, which were used for texts on sarcophagi or tomb and temple walls: such as yellow for wooden objects or green for items made of bronze.

The Rosetta Stone – a Breakthrough

The most important find of the Napoleonic troops in Egypt was a granite block with texts in three different scripts: Greek, demotic and hieroglyphics. It was discovered by soldiers during fortification work in 1799 in Rosetta, a place at the mouth of the western arm of the Nile. The Greek text turned out to be a priestly decree in honour of a king. The French scientists hoped that the other texts would be identical thus enabling them to decipher the two Egyptian texts. However, as they left Egypt with the defeated troops, they were forced to leave all their findings to the English victors, even the important Rosetta Stone. Whilst they had wisely copied the inscriptions, it now seemed they would be forced to relinquish them to the English. However, the French insisted that they would rather destroy all the results of their work, all drawings, copies and notes. Their spokesman threatened the victors with a dramatic comparison: "Think of your place in history," he called, "you too will have burned a library in Alexandria!" The French were allowed to keep their drawings, but it was to be another 20 years before, with the help of the Rosetta

text, the fundamental principles of the Egyptian script could be reconstructed. Many tried, but the decisive breakthrough was made by a Frenchman who was only nine years old when the stone was discovered: Jean François Champollion. He was a linguistic genius, had mastered the basics of Hebrew and Arabic by the time he was 12 years old, studied Coptic and ancient history in Grenoble and was appointed professor when he was only 18. In 1822, in a letter which has since become famous, Champollion published his first findings on the Rosetta text, and it is this year, if any, which marked the beginning of Egyptology as a science. However, it was not just the experts who welcomed and acclaimed Champollion's findings. A growing sector of the public, particularly in France, had been showing interest in Egypt, as well as the Orient. This may have been a result of the complicated nature of revolutionary and economic developments, or because industrialisation and the urban proletariat had nourished a yearning for a realm in which one could recuperate: whether languishing on a plush cushion in the arms of devoted ladies of the harem or in sight of ancient temples emanating order, wisdom and eternity. In France, the fame of Egypt became inextricably linked to that of Napoleon. And so, ironically, it was the military catastrophe of his expedition to Egypt which was to confer on the general and subsequent emperor legendary status, way above any other officer or politician of his time. Vivant Denon, the author and museum director, played a major role in the creation of this legend. Thoughts of Napoleon automatically conjured up images of pyramids and vice versa. Countless chairs, beds, plates, cups and pieces of jewellery were made in the so-called "Empire style" based on Egyptian models, monuments were erected in the shape of pyramids, dresses embellished with Egyptian patterns, and paintings done in the Egyptian style, often based on motifs from the well-circulated "Description de l'Egypte". There was even a tourist trade of sorts. Young aristocrats and sons of wealthy citizens supplemented their obligatory

Grand Tour of Europe with a trip to the Nile. In 1842, a Prussian group had themselves painted with a flag blowing in the wind on top of Cheops' pyramid; in 1869, Empress Eugénie attended the opening of the Suez canal and the première of Verdi's opera "Aida". Early photos show fellahs pulling Europeans up the pyramids. And all brought souvenirs home with them which had been acquired by more or less legal means.

In 1799, near a place called Rosetta, French officers discovered a stele with three inscriptions: one in Greek and two written in hieroglyphs. The victorious English confiscated the stone, but the French had made a copy and Champollion worked with that. He assumed that the texts had the same content, and deciphered the others from the Greek version.
London, British Museum

In the 19th century Egypt became a favourite holiday destination for adventurous, mostly prosperous Europeans. Climbing the pyramids had not yet been forbidden and the locals gladly lent a hand.
Photo by Henri Béchard, around 1880

General shipments to Europe

The fact that those undertaking educational trips in the 19th century were able to familiarise themselves beforehand with Egyptian culture in Europe was thanks to two "consuls" in particular: Bernadino Drovetti and Henry Salt. Drovetti first visited Egypt as an officer in Napoleon's army and Salt, an Englishman, was a travelling companion to wealthy tourists. Protected by diplomatic immunity, assisted by the indifference of the Turkish Governor and with the help of unscrupulous agents, they searched for sarcophagi, statues, papyri and fragments from the walls of temples and tombs. The material was stored in the consulate grounds and then sold to the highest bidding museum. With the works of art they shipped to Europe, Salt and Drovetti founded the large collections in London, Paris, Berlin and Turin. So was this shipment of thousands of often truly monumental works of the pharaonic culture, which was largely motivated by the avarice of many of those involved, evidence that the Egyptians were victims of an international conspiracy to steal from them? The counter-argument to this theory claims that due to proper handling in European museums these treasures were better looked after and preserved than would ever have been possible in Egypt. All too often, Egyptians had misused valuable works of art as building material or broken relics down into handy sizes to sell to tourists. It is also an undeniable fact that it was a European, the Frenchman Auguste Mariette who, commissioned by the Turkish viceroy, ensured that important pieces stayed in the country. In 1858, he became founding director of an Egyptian museum in Bulaq, from which later followed the famous Cairo Museum.

Europe makes amends

In the 19th century, the Europeans were able to help themselves amply to the treasure chambers of Egypt; in the 20th century it was time to make amends. No other country has ever received such large-scale scientific and financial aid for the research and conservation of its own past as Egypt. True, the Europeans were also acting in their own interest, as the roots of their own cultures were derived from the Pharaohs, but it was the Egyptians who profited directly. Even the self-confidence of the modern state rests largely on an inheritance which was discovered by foreigners and protected by the international community.

The world owes the most significant find of the 20th century – the tomb of Tutankhamun – to two Englishmen. One, Howard Carter, was an impoverished painter. Arriving in Egypt on a 17-year commission to copy pictures and inscriptions for tourists, he became increasingly obsessed by the idea that there must still be tombs lying undiscovered in the Valley of the Kings. He gained financial backing to dig there, first from the Americans then, in 1912, from Lord Carnarvon. Lord Carnarvon's first love was horses and cars. Following an accident, however, his doctors had recommended a stay in a hot, dry climate which ultimately led him to Egypt. Carter searched and dug for Carnarvon for ten years until, on 4 November 1922, his luck turned. He told how he arrived at the excavation site to find none of the Egyptian employees working. They had been waiting excitedly to show him steps leading downwards carved in the rock which they had just cleared. Carter ordered them to continue digging until the workers reached a door which had been entirely blocked up with stones. Whilst the door showed signs of earlier tampering, it had been closed with Nile mud and an 18th Dynasty seal, i.e. approximately 3,500 years previously. As yet, no archaeologist had found a rock chamber sealed as early as this in the Valley of the Kings; they had always been beaten to it by tomb robbers. Behind the stone door they found a passage full of rubble. A second sealed door was discovered and opened, and when Carter held a flickering candle into the dark he saw shadows of animals and statues and, from all sides, the reflection of gold. It was an antechamber full to the brim with burial furnishings designed to enhance the king's life in the next world; beds, chairs, weapons, vases, baskets, chests and, flanking the door to the burial chamber, two statues of watchmen. Carter and Carnarvon worked extremely diligently, registering and photographing all objects and, where necessary, conserving them. They were also assisted by some members of the Metropolitan Museum, New York, who just happened to be in Thebes at the time. This work in the antechamber took almost three months to complete, after which Carnarvon's and Carter's workers opened the door to the burial chamber.

They discovered a gilded shrine which almost entirely filled the chamber, the like of which had never been seen by any

A glance into the Valley of the Kings in 1923. The large shaft leads to the tomb of Ramesses VI, and the newly laid wall in the foreground is protecting the entrance into the tomb of Tutankhamun, found the year before. The credit for this must go to two Englishmen, Howard Carter who was financed by Lord Carnarvon. Carter had been searching Egyptian ground for ten years with his patron's money, before he came across the tomb treasure of the pharaoh Tutankhamun.

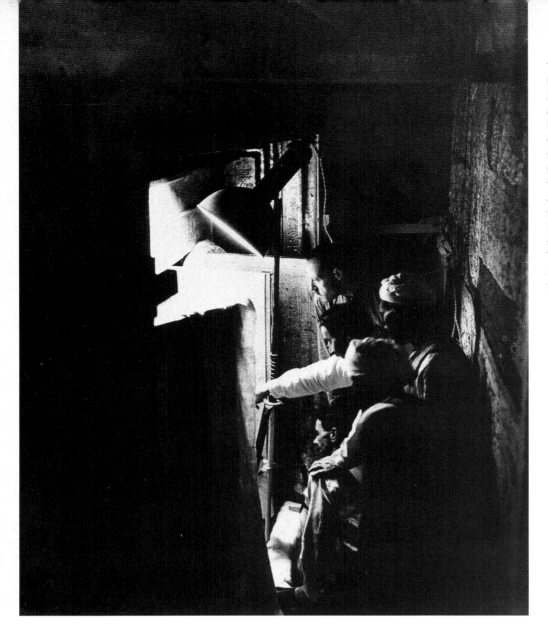

The burial chamber of Tutankhamun had lain in the dark for over 3,000 years and, in contrast to almost all other royal tombs, since his burial nobody had entered it. Only the antechamber had been searched by thieves. Only after Carter had recorded and gathered together the contents of the antechamber did he open the access to the burial chamber and cast the beam of his searchlight on the most significant tomb find in Egypt. That was on 17th February 1923. Howard Carter is seen here between two colleagues.

archaeologist before. This proved to be the outer of four coffins, in which the inner three sarcophagi were fitted, one inside the other, with the final one containing the mummy of King Tutankhamun, his head and upper body covered with a gold mask. It was a sensational find and can now be admired in the Cairo museum. Like the pyramids, it gives a remarkable insight into the royal death cult. The burial chamber was opened in February 1923 and Lord Carnarvon died in April of the same year. Carter needed six years to clear the tomb, ensuring all necessary conservation measures were taken. In 1923, the discovery of the tomb of Tutankhamun was widely reported in the world's press, but a second find of similar significance was to go virtually unmentioned. The French archaeologist, Pierre Montet, discovered the tomb of King Psusennes and other important personalities of the 21st and 22nd Dynasty in the eastern delta of the Nile, near Tanis – all untouched. But this discovery was made in 1939, at the outbreak of World War II when the world was concerned with more important things than pharaohs.

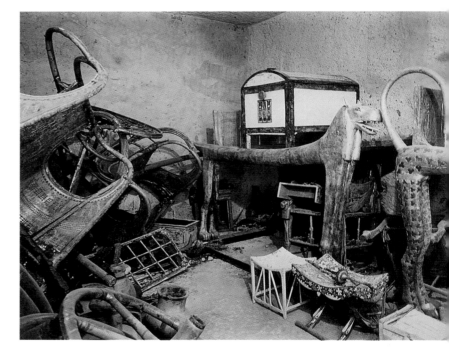

Shortly after Tutankhamun had been buried, thieves had ransacked the antechamber of his tomb, leaving behind the mess that Howard Carter found in November 1922.

Philae, Abu Simbel and the tomb of Nefertari – a Rescue Operation

The second half of the 20th century was less influenced by any further discoveries than by the shifting of the temples of Abu Simbel and Philae. This was made necessary by the building of the new dam, South of Aswan, as otherwise they would have been submerged under the water surface of the resulting reservoir along with several dozen Nubian villages. The inhabitants were relocated by the Egyptian government and the temple was taken care of by the United Nations organisation UNESCO, who financed and organised the relocation of the temples, something which had never been undertaken before.

Located amongst palms on the small island of Philae was an entire temple town from the Late Period, next to which were two Coptic churches, partially built from original temple stones – an image which, to European eyes, must have seemed a particularly harmonious combination of culture and nature – at least until building was started on

To keep tomb paintings, which were threatened by salt and damp, in their original place and simultaneously to be able to show them all over the world – that was the dilemma that the Getty Foundation in California solved. It had the tomb of Nefertari lavishly restored and then photographed the walls so that the most important rooms could be rebuilt to the correct dimensions.

the first Aswan dam in 1902. The dammed water reached almost to the roof of the temple and the island only surfaced again for a few short weeks in summer before the new inundation. Because completion of the new high dam in 1971 meant that the island would have been entirely submerged, the decision was made to transport the most important buildings (without the foundations and Coptic churches) to another island, 600 metres away and 13 metres higher. Unlike Philae, Abu Simbel consisted of two huge rock temples, the larger of which had been hewn 63 metres deep into the rock. On the rear alcove wall the idolised Ramesses II sat on his throne between three gods. Rooms and passages to this rear alcove were orientated such that twice a year, at the equinox, the sun completely lit up the statues of the gods. In front of the entrance four statues were cut out of the rock representing the seated Ramesses, each about 21 metres high. The six statues of Ramesses and his consort Nefertari in front of the temple were also an impressive ten metres high. The figures show which rock masses had to be moved – 64 metres higher and 180 metres further inland. The statues and walls had to be sawn out of the rock, taken apart and then put back together again at the new site, facing exactly the same direction. Heavy-duty dams had to be constructed to protect the building-site from the water which was already rising. The new imitation massif, into which both the smaller and the larger temple were inserted, is made of hollow, concrete couplings covered with sheets of rock. In 1980, the reconstruction of Philae and Abu Simbel was completed and celebrated. Total cost of the rescue operation: 72 million dollars.

Water is not the only danger; the flocks of tourists are also destroying monuments, in particular the wall paintings inside the tombs. Jostling crowds brush against the painted walls which are slowly being worn away, while the warm breath of the visitors turns into condensation on the walls and mixes with the natural salt, resulting in salt crystals which are peeling off the paint layers from underneath. This was the case in the tomb of Nefertari which the Egyptian Antiquities Authority was forced to close. Together with the authorities, the J. Paul Getty Foundation has developed and financed strategies for the greatest possible preservation of the remaining wall paintings. In addition, however, they have photographed the painted walls of individual rooms so that they can be duplicated in their original size, thus in a sense creating a portable tomb. Not as the booty of an art thief, as once was the case, but as a replica – a tomb which can be admired around the globe by all those who may otherwise never have had the chance to experience the culture of Ancient Egypt.

The head of a colossus statue of Ramesses II is suspended on the cables of a crane on its way to the new rock temple of Abu Simbel.

When the Egyptian government built a new dam at Aswan, the reservoir threatened to flood two of the most important ensembles in Egyptian construction history: the island of Philae with the temple of Isis and the two rock temples of Abu Simbel. UNESCO financed this complicated rescue, which was completed in 1980. The statues of the rock temple were brought 180 metres inland and 64 metres higher to an artificially built concrete rock, while the most important buildings of the island of Philae were transported over steel rails onto the island of Agilkia, 13 metres higher.

Illustration, over the page:
The new island of Philae-Agilkia with the temple of Isis, the centre of Ancient Egyptian religion with the longest history. The temple was not closed until the 6th century when the Coptic Christians deconsecrated it. The last Christians retreated from the Mohammedans around the 12th century. Each time, over long periods, members of different denominations worshipped their gods there side by side.

Here, Egyptian history is divided into the periods of rule of the individual kings (pharaohs), the Dynasties (kings from the same family) and the "Kingdoms". Periods of decline are regarded as "Intermediate Periods". The dates are sometimes disputed; we give them under reservation. Not all kings are listed. All dates refer to the period before the birth of Christ, if no other information is given.

Overview of Egyptian History

Pyramid text of Unas

Djoser

Step pyramid at Saqqara

Bent pyramid of Dashur

Prehistory

7000–3000 B.C.
After changes in the climate, more and more nomadic tribes settle on the banks of the Nile. Agriculture, cattle rearing

c. 3000
King Narmer presumably unites the areas of Upper Egypt (Aswan to Cairo) and Lower Egypt (Nile Delta) into one kingdom.
Founding of the state, administration, calendar
Invention of a script
Brick tombs in Abydos

Old Kingdom
2670–2195 (3rd to 6th Dynasty)

3rd Dynasty
Djoser
First monumental stone building:
the Step Pyramid in Saqqara

4th Dynasty
Memphis becomes capital, administration is centralised.
Seneferu builds the Bent Pyramid at Dahshur.
Building of Cheops' pyramid in Giza
Building of Chephren pyramid and the Sphinx in Giza
Building of Mycerinus pyramid

5th Dynasty
Unas builds pyramids, adorns interiors with religious texts:
Pyramid texts
The first wisdom instructions are recorded.

First Intermediate Period
2195–2040 (8th–11th Dynasty)

Anarchy, kingdom in decline, tomb robbing
It is questioned whether the state is the divine order.
Start of a diverse literature, harp songs.

Cheops' pyramid at Giza

Cheops

The Sphinx at Giza

The Blind Harpist

Pharaoh with horse and chariot

Tuthmosis's obelisk

The Valley of the Kings

The Temple at Luxor

Middle Kingdom
2040–1781 (11th–13th Dynasty)

11th Dynasty
Mentuhotep II subjugates local rulers, re-unifies Upper and Lower Egypt and makes Thebes the capital.

12th Dynasty
Amenemhet I–IV
Privately owned land becomes re-nationalised.
Campaigns against Libya and Palestine
Sesostris I–III
Conquests in Nubia
Significant literary works such as the Tale of Sinuhe

Second Intermediate Period
1650–1550 (14th–17th Dynasty)

Rule of the Asian interlopers, the Hyksos, in Lower Egypt (Delta area)
They introduce horses and chariots.

New Kingdom
1550–1075 (18th–20th Dynasty)

18th Dynasty
Amosis, Amenhotep I
Tuthmosis I and II
After driving back the Hyksos expansion, campaigns of conquest as far as Syria and the Euphrates makes Egypt a "world power".
Thebes becomes the capital and Amun the national god.
Temples of Luxor and Karnak, rock tombs in the Valley of the Kings
Hatshepsut
Temple of Deir el-Bahari

Tuthmosis III and IV
Like priests and officials, the military gains influence.

Amenhotep II and III
Kingdom and culture at its peak

Amenhotep IV = Akhenaten
Religious and cultural revolution, transfer of royal residence to Amarna
Tutankhamun
Transfer of royal residence back to Thebes
Horemheb

19th Dynasty
Ramesses I, Seti I
Ramesses II
Great buildings: Karnak, Ramesseum and Abu Simbel.

20th Dynasty
Ramesses III
Unrest in Deir el-Medinah, village of the royal tomb workers

Ramesses IV–X
Ramesses XI
Tomb robbery trials, unrest
Tanis (in the Delta) becomes capital, Thebes under rule of priests

Hatshepsut

The Temple of Deir el-Bahari

Nefertiti

Echnaton

Tutankhamun

Ramesseum

Pashedu's grave

Abu Simbel

Third Intermediate Period
1075–650 (21st–25th Dynasty)

Kingdom in decline

Late Period
664–332 (26th–30th Dynasty)

Libyan, Ethiopian, Persian rulers in Egypt

Ptolemaic Period

Alexander the Great (332–30) conquers Egypt and founds Alexandria, the future intellectual centre of the Mediterranean

Ptolemaic kings
Greek rulers, from Macedonia, installed by Alexander.

310–30
Ptolemy I–XII
Cleopatra I–VI
Temples of Dendera, Esna, Edfu, Kom Ombo, Philae

Cleopatra VII
last Egyptian queen (actually of Greek nationality)
Fire in the library in Alexandria

Rule of the Romans
30 B.C.–395 A.D.

Egypt becomes a Roman province.
391 Caesar Theodosius declares Christianity the national religion, most Egyptian temples are closed.

Byzantine rule
394–640 A.D

Egypt is ruled from Constantinople.
550 A.D.: Closure of the Isis temple of Philae

Arabic-Moslem rule

640 A.D.: Expulsion of the Byzantines. Egypt becomes a province of the caliph kingdom.

Cleopatra

Philae

Courtyard at Edfu

In Tutankhamun's grave

Index – Persons

Index – Monuments and Tombs

Bibliography

Arnold, Dieter, Lanny Bell and Bjerre Ragnhild Finnestad (eds.): Temples of Ancient Egypt, Ithaca NY 1997

Aldred, Cyril: Egyptian Art, London 1980

Assmann, Jan: Ägyptische Hymnen und Gebete, Zurich 1975

Bierbrier, Morris L.: The Tomb-builders of the Pharaohs, London 1982/Cairo 1989

Brunner Hellmut: Die Weisheitsbücher der Ägypter, Lehren für das Leben, Zurich/Munich 1991

Brunner-Traut, Emma: Die Alten Ägypter, Verborgenes Leben unter den Pharaonen, Stuttgart 1981

Brunner-Traut, Emma: Altägyptische Märchen, Mythen und andere volkstümliche Erzählungen, Cologne 1991

Description de l'Égypte, publiée par les ordres de Napoléon Bonaparte. Reprint of the illustrated volumes, Cologne 1998

Desroches Noblecourt, Christiane: La Femme au temps des Pharaons, Paris 1986

Donadoni-Roveri, Anna Maria (ed.): Das Alte Ägypten, 3 vols.: Das Alltagsleben/Die religiösen Vorstellungen/Kunst als Fest, Milan 1987

Dunand, Françoise and Roger Lichtenberg: Mummies, A Journey Through Eternity, London s. a.

Eggebrecht, Arne (ed.): Das Alte Ägypten, 3000 Jahre Geschichte und Kultur des Pharaonenreiches, Munich 1988

Fahkry, A.: The Pyramids, Chicago/London 1969

Flamarion, Edith: Cleopatra, The Life and Death of a Pharaoh, New York 1997

Gardiner, Sir Alan: Egyptian Grammar, Oxford 1927/1988

Germer, Renate: Mumien, Zeugen des Pharaonenreiches, Zurich/Munich 1991

Germer, Renate (ed.): Mummies. Life After Death in Ancient Egypt, Munich/New York 1997

Gutgesell, Manfred: Arbeiter und Pharaonen, Wirtschafts- und Sozialgeschichte im Alten Ägypten, Hildesheim 1989

Helck, Wolfgang (ed.): Lexikon der Ägyptologie, 6 vols., Wiesbaden 1972 ff.

Helck, Wolfgang and Eberhard Otto: Kleines Wörterbuch der Ägyptologie, Wiesbaden 1987

Herodotus: Histories, 2 vols., translated by George Rawlinson, edited by E. H. Blakeney, introduction by John Warrington

Hornung, Erik: Conceptions of God in Ancient Egypt: The One and the Many, Ithaca NY 1996

Hornung, Erik: Geist der Pharaonenzeit, Munich 1992

Hornung, Erik: Tal der Könige, Die Ruhestätte der Pharaonen, Zurich 1982

Kemp, Barry John: Ancient Egypt. Anatomy of a Civilization, New York 1993

Leclant, Jean (ed.): Le Monde égyptien, 3 volumes: I. Le Temps des pyramides, Paris 1978; II. L'empire des conquérants, Paris 1979; III. L'Egypte du crépuscule, Paris 1980

Lichtheim, Miriam: Ancient Egyptian Literature, A Book of Readings, 3 vols., Berkeley/Los Angeles/London 1980

Manniche, Lise: Sexual Life in Ancient Egypt, London/New York 1987

Mekhitarian, Arpag: Egyptian Painting, New York 1978

Montet, Pierre: La Vie quotidienne en Égypte au temps des Ramsès, Paris 1946

Omlin, Jos. A.: Der Papyrus 55Lz11d1001 und seine satirisch-erotischen Zeichnungen und Inschriften, Turin 1973

Peck, William H. and J. G. Ross: Drawings from Ancient Egypt, London 1978

Quirke, Stephen and Jeffrey Spencer (eds.): British Museum: The British Museum Book of Ancient Egypt, London 1992

Robins, Gay: Women in Ancient Egypt, London 1993

Romer, John: Ancient Lives, London 1981

Schlott, Adelheid: Schrift und Schreiber im Alten Ägypten, Munich 1989

Schlögl, Hermann A.: Amenophis IV. Echnaton, Reinbek 1986

Schlögl, Hermann A.: Ramses II., Reinbek 1993

Schmitz, Bettina und Ute Steffgen (eds.): Waren sie nur schön? Frauen im Spiegel der Jahrtausende, Mainz 1998

Schott, Siegfried: Altägyptische Liebeslieder, Zurich 1950

Schüssler, Karlheinz: Die Ägyptischen Pyramiden, Erforschung, Baugeschichte und Bedeutung, Cologne 1983

Simoën, Jean-Claude: Égypte éternelle, les voyageurs photographes au siècle dernier, Paris 1993

Stadelmann, Rainer: Die ägyptischen Pyramiden: Vom Ziegelbau zum Weltwunder, Mainz 1985

Stierlin, Henri: The Pharaohs' Master-Builders, Paris 1995

Stierlin, Henri: The Gold of the Pharaohs, Paris 1997

Tompkins, Peter: Secrets of the Great Pyramid, New York 1973

Vercoutter, Jean: The Search for Ancient Egypt, New York 1973

Vernus, Pascal: Affaires et scandales sous les Ramsès, La crise des valeurs dans l'Égypte du Nouvel-Empire, Paris 1993

Wildung, Dietrich: Egypt. From Prehistory to the Romans, Cologne 1997

Museum and collection catalogues:

Ägyptisches Museum Berlin der Staatlichen Museen Preußischer Kulturbesitz, Berlin 1989

Ägyptisches Museum Museumsinsel, Staatliche Museen zu Berlin, Stiftung Preußischer Kulturbesitz, Mainz 1991

Ancient Egyptian Art in the Brooklyn Museum, New York 1989

Le Louvre, Les Antiquités Égyptiennes, Paris 1990

Museo Egizio di Torino, Milan 1989

The Egyptian Museum Cairo, Official Catalogue, Mainz, 1987

The Luxor Museum of Ancient Egyptian Art, Guidebook, Cairo 1978

Exhibition catalogues:

Das Alte Reich, Ägypten im Zeitalter der Pyramiden, Roemer- und Pelizaeus-Museum, Hildesheim 1986

Götter – Pharaonen, Villa Hügel, Essen 1978

In the Tomb of Nefertari, Conservation of the Wall Paintings, The J. Paul Getty Museum and the Getty Conservation Institute, Santa Monica 1992

La Magia in Egitto ai Tempi dei Faraoni, Mantova 1991

Nofret die Schöne, vol. 1: Die Frau im Alten Ägypten, Munich/Berlin 1985, vol. 2: Wahrheit und Wirklichkeit, Hildesheim 1985

Schönheit – Abglanz der Göttlichkeit, Kosmetik im Alten Ägypten, Ingolstadt/Munich/Berlin 1990

Suche nach Unsterblichkeit, Totenkult und Jenseitsglaube im Alten Ägypten, Roemer- und Pelizaeus-Museum, Hildesheim 1990

Tutanchamun, Berlin, Ägyptisches Museum der Staatlichen Museen Preußischer Kulturbesitz, Mainz 1980

Egyptian Collections and Museums

Austria

Vienna
Kunsthistorisches Museum
Burgring 5
1010 Wien

Belgium

Brussels
Musées Royaux d'Art et d'Histoire/
Koninklijke Musea voor Kunst en Geschiedenis
Parc du Cinquantenaire 10
1000 Bruxelles

Morlanwelz-Mariemont
Musée royal de Mariemont
100 Chaussée de Mariemont
7140 Morlanwelz-Mariemont

Brazil

Rio de Janeiro
Museu Nacional
Universidade Federal de Rio de Janeiro
Quinta da Boa Vista São Cristovão
20000 Rio de Janeiro

Canada

Toronto
Royal Ontario Museum
100 Queen's Park
Toronto
Ontario M5S 2C6

Croatia

Zagreb
Archeological Museum – Zagreb
Trg Nikole Šubića Zrinskog 19
10000 Zagreb

Czech Republic

Prague
Náprstkovo muzeum asijských, afrických a amerických kultur
Betlémské námesti 1
110 00 Praha 1

Denmark

Copenhagen
Ny Carlsberg Glyptotek
Dantes Plads 7
1556 København

Nationalmuseet
Frederiksholms Kanal 12
1220 København K.

Egypt

Alexandria
Greco-Roman Museum
Museum Street
21521 Alexandria

Aswan
Assuan Museum
Elephantine Island
Aswan

Cairo
Egyptian Museum
11556 Midan el-Tahrir
Misr al-Kahira

Luxor
Luxor Museum
Cornish Street
al-Uksur

France

Amiens
Musée de Picardie
48 Rue de la République
80000 Amiens

Avignon
Musée Calvet
65 Rue Joseph-Vernet
84000 Avignon

Lyon
Musée des Beaux-Arts
Palais St. Pierre
20 Place des Terreaux
69001 Lyon

Marseille
Musée d'Archéologie Méditerranéenne
Centre de la Vieille Charité
2, Rue de la Vieille Charité
13002 Marseille

Paris
Musée du Louvre
34–36 Quai du Louvre
75058 Paris

Roanne
Musée Joseph-Déchelette
22 Rue Anatole-France
42300 Roanne

Strasbourg
Musée de l'Art Égyptien
Palais Universitaire
67000 Strasbourg

Toulouse
Musée Georges Labit
43 Rue des Martyrs de la Libération
31400 Toulouse

Germany

Berlin
Ägyptisches Museum und Papyrussammlung
Schloßstr. 70
14059 Berlin and
Bodestraße 1–3
10178 Berlin
(There are plans to combine these two museums and move them to the "Museumsinsel")

Frankfurt
Liebighaus
Museum Alter Plastik
Schaumainkai 71
60596 Frankfurt

Hanover
Kestner-Museum
Trammplatz 3
30159 Hannover

Heidelberg
Sammlung des Ägyptologischen Instituts
Universität Heidelberg
Marstallhof 4
69117 Heidelberg

Hildesheim
Roemer- und Pelizaeus-Museum
Am Steine 1–2
31134 Hildesheim

Leipzig
Ägyptisches Museum der Universität Leipzig
Schillerstraße 6
04109 Leipzig

Munich
Staatliche Sammlung Ägyptischer Kunst
Hofgartenstraße 1 (Residenz)
80539 München

Tübingen
Ägyptische Sammlung der Universität
Schloß Hohentübingen
72070 Tübingen

Würzburg
Martin-von-Wagner-Museum der Universität Würzburg
Antikensammlung
Tor A
Residenz
97070 Würzburg

Great Britain

Birmingham
Birmingham Museum and Art Gallery
Chamberlain Square
Birmingham B3 3DH

Cambridge
Fitzwilliam Museum
Trumpington Street
Cambridge CB2 1RB

Edinburgh
Royal Museum of Scotland
Chambers Street
Edinburgh EH1 1JF

Glasgow
Hunterian Museum
University of Glasgow
University Avenue
Glasgow G12 8QQ

Liverpool
Liverpool Museum
William Brown Street
Liverpool L3 8EN

London
British Museum
Great Russell Street
London WC1B 3DG

Petrie Museum of Egyptian
Archaeology
University College
Gower Street
London WC1E 6BT

Manchester
Manchester Museum
University of Manchester
Oxford Road
Manchester M13 9PL

Oxford
Ashmolean Museum of Art and
Archaeology
Beaumont Street
Oxford OX1 2PH

Swansea
Wellcome Museum of Antiquities
University of Wales Swansea
Singleton Park
Swansea SA2 8PP

Hungary

Budapest
Szépűvészeti Múzeum
Egyiptomi osztály
Dózsa György út 41
1396 Budapest 62

Israel

Jerusalem
Israel Museum
P. O. Box 71117
91710 Jerusalem

Italy

Bologna
Museo Civico Archeologico
Via Dell'Archinginnasio 2
40124 Bologna

Florence
Museo Archeologico
Via della Colonna 36
50121 Firenze

Milan
Museo d'Arte Antica
Castello Sforzesco
20121 Milano

Naples
Museo Archeologico Nazionale
Piazza Museo 19
80135 Napoli

Rome
Monumenti, Musei e Gallerie
Pontificie
Museo Gregoriano Egizio
Viale Vaticano
00120 Cittá del Vaticano

Turin
Museo Egizio
Via Accademia delle Scienze 6
10123 Torino

Netherlands

Amsterdam
Allard Pierson Museum
Archeologisch Museum van de
Universiteit van Amsterdam
Oude Turfmarkt 127
1012 GC Amsterdam

Leiden
Stichting Rijksmuseum van
Oudheden
Rapenburg 28
2311 EW Leiden

Poland

Cracow
Muzeum Narodowe w Krakowie
Ulice Pilsudskiego 12
31–109 Kraków

Warsaw
Muzeum Narodowe w Warszawie
Aleje Jerozolimskie 3
00–495 Warszawa

Portugal

Lisbon
Museu Calouste Gulbenkian
Avenida de Berna 45 A
1093 Lisboa

Russia

Moskow
Pushkin Museum
Ulica Volchonka 12
121019 Moskva

St. Petersburg
The Hermitage
Dvorcovaja Naberežnaja 34–36
191065 St. Petersburg

Sweden

Stockholm
Medelhavsmuseet
Fredsgatan 2
Box 5405
11484 Stockholm

Uppsala
Museum för Klassika Fornsaker
Gustavianum
75220 Uppsala

Switzerland

Basle
Museum für Völkerkunde
Augustinergasse 2
4001 Basel

Geneva
Musée d'art et d'historie
2, Rue Charles-Galland
C. P. 3432
1211 Genève 3

Spain

Barcelona
Museu Arqueológic
Parque de Montjuich
08004 Barcelona

Madrid
Museu Arqueológico Nacional
Calle de Serrano 13
28001 Madrid

Sudan

Khartoum
Sudan National Museum for
Antiquities
El Neel Avenue
P. O. Box 178
Khartoum

United States of America

Baltimore
Walters Art Gallery
600 N. Charles Street
Baltimore
Maryland 21201

Berkeley
Phoebe Hearst Museum of
Anthropology
103 Kroeber Hall #3712
University of California
Berkeley
California 94720–3712

Boston
Museum of Fine Arts
465 Huntington Avenue
Boston
Massachusetts 02115

Brooklyn
The Brooklyn Museum
2000 Eastern Parkway
Brooklyn
New York 11238–6052

Chicago
Oriental Institute Museum
University of Chicago
1155 East 58th Street
Chicago
Illinois 60637

Cleveland
Cleveland Museum of Art
11150 East Boulevard
Cleveland
Ohio 44106

Los Angeles
Los Angeles County Museum of Art
5905 Wilshire Boulevard
Los Angeles
California 90036

Memphis
Art Museum
The University of Memphis Campus
3750 Norriswood Avenue
Memphis
Tennessee 38152

New York
The Metropolitan Museum of Art
5th Avenue at 82nd Street
New York
New York 10028

Philadelphia
University of Pennsylvania Museum
of Archaeology & Anthropology
33rd and Spruce Streets
Philadelphia
Pennsylvania 19104 6324

Princeton
The Art Museum
Princeton University
Princeton
New Jersey 08544–1018

Richmond
Virginia Museum of Fine Arts
2800 Grove Avenue
Richmond
Virginia 23221–2472

Seattle
Seattle Art Museum
100 University Street
P. O. Box 22000
Seattle
Washington 98101

Photographic Credits

The publishers would like to thank the museums, archives and photographers for granting permission for reproductions and for their friendly support while we were working on this book.

Hans Christian Adam, Göttingen: 226 bottom

Ägyptisches Museum der Universität Leipzig: 160

Archiv für Kunst und Geschichte, Berlin/Werner Forman: 54, 100, 106 top, 179

Axiom, London/James Morris (photos): 2, 8–9, 75, 91 top, 171, 174 top, 197 bottom

Bibliothèque nationale de France, Paris: 16 bottom, 18, 208, 211, 217

Bildagentur Schuster/Altitude, Yann Arthus-Bertrand (photo): 24

The British Museum, London: 20, 64 top, 84, 128 bottom, 166 bottom, 167, 185 top, 201, 204, 223

The Brooklyn Museum of Art, Brooklyn NY: 87, 115

Deutsches Apotheken-Museum im Heidelberger Schloß: 213 top left

The Fitzwilliam Museum, Cambridge: 86

The Griffith Institute, Ashmolean Museum, Cambridge: 145 top

Gustav-Lübcke-Museum, Hamm: 213 bottom

Courtesy of the Getty Conservation Trust, Los Angeles, © The J. Paul Getty Trust: 94, 227

Claus & Liselotte Hansmann Kulturgeschichtliches Bildarchiv, Munich: 180, 218

Kestner-Museum, Hanover: 78 left
IFAO, Cairo: 210

The Image Bank, Düsseldorf (photo: Guilian Colliva): 230–231

Lois Lammerhuber, Baden: 12–13

Lehnert & Landrock, Cairo: Endpaper, 16 centre

Jürgen Liepe, Berlin: 22 top, 22 bottom, 26, 30, 42 top, 46, 58 top, 61 top, 65, 69 bottom, 81 top, 85, 93 left, 93 right, 96 left, 98–99 bottom, 111 bottom, 114 top, 114 bottom, 124 top, 130 bottom, 133 top, 134 centre, 139 top, 144 bottom, 146, 148, 154, 158, 162, 163, 164, 169, 170 left, 172, 175, 178 right, 183 right, 184, 186 top, 186 bottom, 202 top, 206 left, 206 right

The Manchester Museum, Manchester: 212

The Metropolitan Museum of Art, New York, photograph © 1989/92 The Metropolitan Museum of Art: 96–97, 187 bottom

Museo Egizio di Torino, Turin: 61 bottom, 80 bottom, 81 bottom, 89, 130 top, 134 bottom, 136 bottom

Pelizaeus-Museum, Hildesheim: 56 top, 71, 82 top, 82 bottom, 88 top, 113, 147 top, 149, 150, 151, 152 top, 155, 170 right

Private collection: 52, 213 right top, 215 top

Rheinisches Bildarchiv, Cologne: 51 bottom, 193, 224

Rijksmuseum van Oudheden, Leiden: 59 bottom, 120 left, 136 top, 145 bottom

RMN, Paris: 107 (photo: Hervé Lewandowski), 112 (photo: B. Hatala), 116, 152 bottom (photos: Chuzeville), 220–221 (photo: Gérard Blot)

Skira, Milan: 105, 109, 110 right, 111 top, 128 top, 129, 132, 182

Staatliche Museen zu Berlin – Preußischer Kulturbesitz, Ägyptisches Museum und Papyrussammlung: 99 top, 104 top, 106 left, 134 top, 140 top, 181 right
Staatliche Museen zu Berlin – Preußischer Kulturbesitz, Kunstbibliothek: 219

Staatliche Sammlung Ägyptischer Kunst, Munich: 197 top

Georg Stärk, Horgen: 18–19

Henri Stierlin, Geneva: 6, 35, 38, 50, 53, 78 right, 121 right, 153, 174 bottom, 187 top, 194, 196, 198 left, 199, 205 bottom, 207

Sygma, Paris: 215 bottom

Frank Teichmann, Stuttgart: 21 top, 29 bottom, 69 top, 117, 183 left, 192 right

Eberhard Thiem, Kaufbeuren: 10–11, 14, 23, 27, 28, 29 top, 31, 32, 33, 37, 40, 41 top, 41 bottom, 42 bottom, 43, 44 left, 44 right, 45, 47, 48, 49, 51 top, 56, 57 top, 57 bottom, 58 bottom, 59 top, 60 top, 62, 63, 64 bottom, 66, 68 top, 72, 74 left, 74 right, 76, 77, 79, 80 top, 83, 88 bottom, 90, 91 bottom, 92 top, 96 bottom, 98 top, 101, 102, 104 bottom, 108, 110 left, 118 left, 118 right, 119, 120 right, 121 left, 122, 123, top, 123 bottom, 125, 126, 131, 133 bottom, 135, 137, 138, 139 centre, 140 bottom, 141, 142, 144 top, 147 bottom, 156, 159, 161, 165, 166 top, 168, 176, 177, 178 left, 181 left, 185 bottom, 188, 191, 195 top, 200 left, 200 right, 203, 205 top, 225, 226 top

UNESCO, Paris: 228, 229

Victoria & Albert Museum, London, Picture Library: 190 bottom

Dietrich Wildung, Berlin: 21 bottom, 68 bottom, 92 bottom, 195 bottom